# Dorchester through the ages

## Foreword

When the tenth volume of the Victoria County History of Oxfordshire appeared, Alan Everitt, Professor of English Local History at Leicester University, wrote a stimulating and memorable review of it called 'The Banburys of England'. 'The long account of Banbury in this volume', he observed, 'is particularly welcome; for the town displays in its classic form many of the features of a certain kind of market centre during most of its history'.

Everitt's judgement was in line with the tradition of the 'Leicester School' of local history, still the only school of its kind in the country. Local history is not concerned simply with what happened in England as revealed by local sources. It is concerned simply with communities within their changing physical and built environments, how they come into existence, develop and change, cohere, erode or disintegrate. The more deeply it is studied, the more it will illuminate accepted outlines of national history. Yet it is a worthy study in itself for teams of people as well as for individuals.

In his review Everitt also noted that although Oxfordshire is one of the smallest counties in England, it has produced more County History volumes than any other county in England, except Wiltshire, which is nearly twice its size, and he praised the University of Oxford for its 'enlightened patronage'.

Within the University of Oxford the main centre of local studies has always been the Department for External Studies and its predecessor, and as a historian who has been equally interested in local history and in education I am glad to have the opportunity of writing a foreword to this interesting and illuminating book which begins with archaeological research and ends with contemporary speculation. The authors explain why Dorchester, increasingly visited by tourists, deserves to have its history properly told. As always in such studies the detail is often fascinating in its own right. Yet the themes are not just local. It is from studies of this kind, indeed, that we can learn how England came to be what it is — with communications and religion figuring prominently.

Rightly the book begins with the physical environment. Historians have to be geographers just as geographers have to concern themselves very directly with history. And no one has made the relationship clearer than Trevor Rowley,

one of its editors, in his *Villages in the Landscape*. Most 20th century visitors to the Abbey will be interested in the River Thames and the Chilterns as well, so near to London in miles and yet so far away. It is appropriate also that geography figures in the ending which, of course, is artificial, for the community continues to change and to develop. The effects of the building of the by-pass are rightly picked out. At beginning and end, therefore, we need a map.

G.M. Young, who was sensitive to landscapes, mental as well as physical, called historians high priests of continuity. This study of Dorchester is a study both of continuity and of discontinuity, and it deserves a wide readership. I am glad that Oxford's Department for External Studies, in line with the tradition identified by Everitt, has chosen to be its publisher.

Asa Briggs.

*The Provost's Lodgings
Worcester College, Oxford.*

1

# Acknowledgements

**DORCHESTER THROUGH THE AGES** has been produced for two reasons. The first is that Dorchester-on-Thames and its surrounding region has been the site of virtually continuous human occupation for the last 6000 years, making it amongst the most important archaeological and historical areas in Britain. The second reason is that, until now, information about Dorchester's past has been scattered throughout a variety of publications; it therefore seemed highly desirable to bring it all together to make a single, well-illustrated account.

Oxford University's Department for External Studies undertook the role of publisher as a reflection of the role which part and full-time staff of the Department have played, over the last 15 years, in helping to piece together the history of this small Oxfordshire village. This work has included survey, excavation, and the organisation of conferences and publications. The production of this book has been a co-operative effort fairly reflecting an extra-mural department's keen interest in the community, past and present. We believe that the selfless cooperation of so many individuals to produce the book is a measure of the affection we all feel for Dorchester and hope that as a consequence of its publication Dorchester's history will become known to a much wider audience. Although during the Roman period and perhaps again during the early Middle Ages Dorchester was a town, for much of its history it has been a village and consequently we refer to it thus.

A large number of people have contributed in one way or another to the production of this book. Some of them are authors of sections, and their names accordingly appear under the relevant headings in the text. In order to avoid duplication and produce a more even text we have taken some liberties with individual contributions and moved small sections from one chapter to another. We would particularly like to thank Richard Bradley, Richard Chambers and David Miles, whose names do not appear in the text, but who played a major role in advising on the archaeological content of the book. There are also many people and institutions who have helped in other ways and we would like to take this opportunity to thank them for their support and encouragement. They are: Dorchester Abbey Authorities, Dorchester Museum Committee, Rosalie Bloxam, Shirley Hermon, Ken Richmond, Linda Rowley, Dick Smethurst, Geoffrey Thomas, Mike Smith, Oxfordshire Museum Services.

## Illustrations

For the provision of illustrations and for permission to reproduce material in their possession, acknowledgement is made to the Ashmolean Library for illustrations on pages 20 and 21; Ashmolean Museum (pages 10, 14, 15, 17, 18, 23 lower, 28, 31 lower, 36); British Library (page 47); British Museum (pages 15, 23 upper, 48); Cambridge University Committee for Aerial Photography (page 3); Institute of Historical Research, University of London (page 41); Oxford Archaeological Unit (pages 7, 29, 31 upper); Oxfordshire County Libraries (pages 19, 51, 53, 55, 70); Oxfordshire Museum Services (pages 32 lower, 52, 57); Oxfordshire Record Society (pages 34 and 35); Public Record Office (page 40); Royal Archaeological Institute and Professor S. S. Frere (page 32, upper illustrations); Society of Antiquaries (page 33, photo by Dr Tania Dickinson).

Maps on pages 4, 5, 9, 10, 11, 17, 22, 24, 25, 30, 33, 37, 38, 45, 49, 50, 59 and 71 are by James Bond. Drawings on pages 6, 12, 13, 14, 15 and 28 are by Mélanie Steiner; the drawing on page 8 is by Jeffrey Wallis. Photographs between pages 60 and 69 are by Dr Malcolm Airs.

*Dorchester from the air, looking north.*

# Introduction

**Trevor Rowley**

This book is about the history of Dorchester from the earliest appearance of man to the present day. To many visitors Dorchester-on-Thames means the Abbey Church and the picturesque buildings which make up the High Street. What is not so well-known is that Dorchester lies at the heart of an area of unparalleled archaeological and historical interest. With the help of the spade and the written record scholars have been working over the past century to unravel Dorchester's unique story, so that it is now possible to trace the prehistory and history of man's activity in this small section of the Thames Valley from its beginnings in the Old Stone Age up to the present time.

Dorchester's role as a centre of human activity over many thousands of years can in part be attributed to its geography. At Dorchester the River Thames, which has lazily made its way southwards from Oxford across its broad flood plain, comes into contact with the Sinodun Hills. These low but prominent hills are an outcrop of the chalk deposits which form the Chiltern Hills to the east of the Thames and to the south stretch from the Berkshire Downs to the south coast of England. At the point of contact the river swerves abruptly eastwards to Wallingford, before it cuts its way through the chalk at the Goring Gap. The distinctive, tree-capped Sinodun Hills are known as the Wittenham Clumps, and form a well-known landmark in the otherwise flat Thames floodplain; as such they must have been used as a guide for travellers in this part of England from the earliest times. Indeed, those people travelling along a north/south axis would have been obliged to ford the Thames close to Dorchester in order to avoid a lengthy eastern detour which would also have meant crossing the River Thame, which joins the Thames just to the south of the village.

3

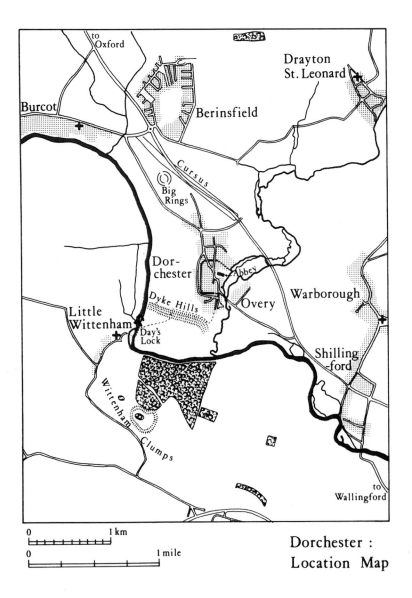

Dorchester :
Location Map

Throughout Dorchester's history the River Thames played an important part in the life of the area as a barrier, a boundary and, paradoxically, a link. The river was navigable from its estuary to beyond Oxford up until the Middle Ages. This meant the possibility of contact and at times conflict with distant places, both within England and along the coastlands of northern Europe.

The rivers in the immediate vicinity of Dorchester form a roughly rectangular promontory of alluvium through which many people had to pass. It is, therefore, little wonder that Dorchester attracted man from the earliest times and that in antiquity it was clearly treated as a special place where great prehistoric monuments were built, and where events of great historical importance took place.

The underlying rocks in this section of the Thames Valley are Upper Greensand and Gault Clay, laid down in the Cretaceous period, some 136-65 million years ago. These rocks are, however, covered by much more recent deposits resulting from glacial and river action. The absence of good local building stone has been a recurring theme in Dorchester's story. During the Roman period limestone was brought in from a few kilometres to the north to build the town walls. Later the medieval Abbey church was also built of stone. Flint from the nearby chalk has been used when feasible, but by itself it is normally an impracticable building material. Otherwise until recently the majority of buildings in and around Dorchester have been constructed from timber and cob. This is mud mixed with animal hair, straw or some other binding agent and has a long history of use in this part of the Thames Valley. It was certainly employed during prehistory and in the Romano-British period, although there is little surviving evidence for it. During the Anglo-Saxon period a series of cob dwellings built on low stone sills were constructed, and it would appear that later a proportion of the medieval Abbey outbuildings were constructed using this material. In 1972 an early medieval cob house

4

was excavated under the 13th century ramparts of Wallingford Castle. There are still several known mud-walled structures in Dorchester today — for instance there is a stretch of wall bounding the road leaving the town to the north, and a curious square hut in the grounds of Bishop's Court. Both are thatched and provide some indication of what many of the buildings in early Dorchester might have looked like.

In this part of Britain the Thames Valley marked the southernmost limit of the ice. At intervals, called interglacials, the climate grew warmer and the ice sheets retreated so that plants and animals were able to recolonise the land. The last ice sheets finally withdrew about 10,500 years ago; the landscape we see today is largely a product of what has happened in the wake of that retreat.

As the ice receded the alternate freezing and thawing of the ground caused considerable weathering of the rocks to the south of the ice mass in the upper reaches of the Thames and in the Cotswolds. During a series of interglacials eroded rock debris was washed down and often carried some distance by the waters of an earlier Upper Thames system. As the river fanned out, the water, flowing in a maze of rivulets, slowed down and deposited debris in the form of deep layers of sand and gravel. As the river system gradually developed it cut itself deeper into the gravel, creating a series of low terraces. Gravel terraces along the Upper Thames provided well-drained sites for settlement from early times and are amongst the richest archaeological areas in the country. There is evidence to show that man was present even during the creation of the terraces, in the form of flint tools and the remains of the animals which he hunted, buried deep down in the gravel.

At this stage there were no permanent settlements; hunters were passing through the area on a seasonal basis in pursuit of their prey. Subsequently, however, there is evidence of almost continuous and often extensive human occupation extending over

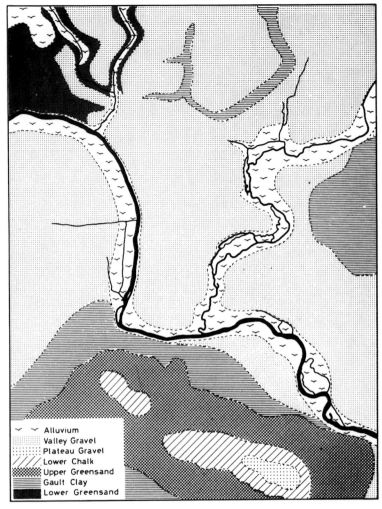

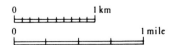

Alluvium
Valley Gravel
Plateau Gravel
Lower Chalk
Upper Greensand
Gault Clay
Lower Greensand

Dorchester :
Drift Geology

0          1 km

0                    1 mile

at least 6000 years. It was during this most recent phase that man fashioned the Dorchester landscape in the form we know it today. Indeed, most of what we see is the product of the last 1000 years and much of what we see outside the ancient earthworks and buildings is even more recent. The reason for this is the gravel itself. Gravel is one of the most important sources of aggregate in Britain, used in road construction and for concrete. Commercial quarrying for gravel has been a feature of the Dorchester area for at least the last 50 years, so much so that most of the accessible gravel reserves close to Dorchester are already exhausted. The large scale gravel-winning operations, which have been a dominant characteristic of the Dorchester scene since the end of World War II, have left behind a landscape of man-made lakes and reconstituted agricultural land. In the process much of the early history of man has been destroyed. Here is a paradox: gravel extraction reveals the history of man in Dorchester at the same time as it systematically destroys it. This situation led to the publication of a survey of the archaeological sites of the Upper Thames Valley in 1974 by Benson and Miles which detailed the threats to archaeological sites and suggested specific policies for survey, excavation and selective preservation. Dorchester and its surrounding area was highlighted as an area of outstanding importance where every effort should be made to conserve the surviving archaeological sites and monuments.

Cropmarks are particularly important in prehistoric and Romano-British studies, but they can also be vital to the understanding of post-Roman landscapes. Cropmarks are features normally only visible from the air, in the form of differential markings in fields

carrying a cereal crop. Generally these marks represent either areas where the crop is riper and thus more bleached than the rest of the crop, or where it is less ripe and therefore much greener. Such marks are normally a function of the subsoil, principally of its depth and richness and the amount of available moisture. Darker lines may indicate the presence of filled ditches, where deep root penetration leads to slow ripening plants; lighter lines will reflect wall foundations or roads, where resistance to growth results in less luxuriant plants which ripen earlier than the main crop. Cropmarks result from ditched or buried features whose earthworks have been ploughed out, and as such they represent an erased landscape which nevertheless may have existed in earthwork form not long ago. It is, therefore, just as important to record and understand these features, which often bear little relation to the modern landscape, as it is to record surviving earthworks.

The Dorchester area is particularly fortunate to have been the subject of intensive aerial reconnaissance since the 1920s. As a result several important collections of aerial photographs have been built up and are available for analysis. If further sites are not to

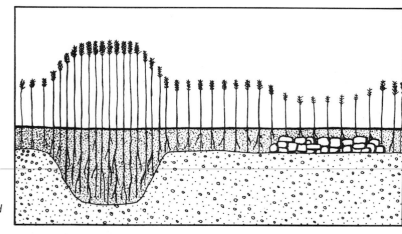

*How cropmarks are formed: later ripening and more vigorous growth over a ditch contrasts with stunted growth and parching over a buried wall.*

be lost without record as a consequence of modern development careful plotting of information shown up by aerial surveys on to maps is an essential task.

Other techniques which archaeologists have used to identify sites in the area around Dorchester include fieldwalking and geophysical surveying. These essential, if often laborious, tasks will pinpoint sites on the ground and sometimes give an indication of what they contain. Normally excavation is only undertaken as a final resort if the site is to be destroyed or severely damaged. Such investigation is known as 'rescue archaeology'. Over the past 50 years there have been a considerable number of major excavations in and around Dorchester. However, the first professional investigation was undertaken on Dyke Hills a century ago, by one of the great pioneers of British archaeology, General Pitt-Rivers. Subsequently excavations have been directed by A.H.A. Hogg and C.E. Stephens on the Roman defences of Dorchester, by Professor Richard Atkinson on the great prehistoric henge and other ritual monuments to the north-west of Dorchester; Professor Sheppard Frere, Trevor Rowley and Richard Bradley have all excavated inside the Roman and Saxon settlement, and more recently Richard Chambers and David Miles of the Oxford Archaeological Unit have excavated a wide range of sites ahead of gravel-digging and the construction of the Dorchester bypass. In addition there have been numerous smaller investigations and chance finds. This formidable history of archaeological work has meant that Dorchester has received more attention than any comparable area in the Thames valley and this has helped us to build up a detailed picture of the evolution of this small region.

The work of the archaeologist has been complemented by that of the historian, whose examination of surviving written records has allowed the history of Dorchester over the past 1400 years to be written. The most comprehensive history appears in the *Victoria County History, Oxfordshire*, Volume VII. The final source of evidence is in the buildings themselves and architectural historians have

analysed the structure and fabric of Dorchester's houses and Abbey church to complete the picture. Thus we are able to trace Dorchester's story from its first inhabitants to the present day — a story which involves an important prehistoric religious centre, two major prehistoric fortifications, a Roman fort and town, an early Christian cathedral and a medieval abbey. In the following pages you will find Dorchester's story told by some of the people who have been most closely involved in analysing the archaeology and history of this unique area.

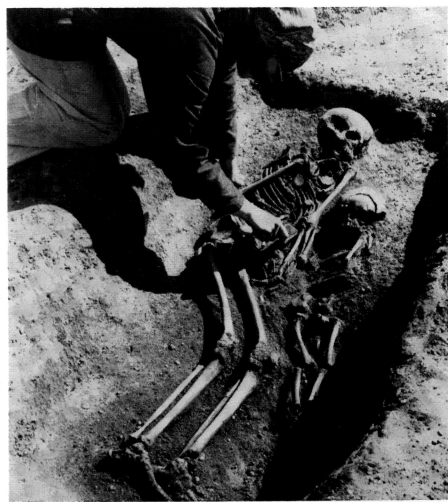

*Excavation of a grave at the pagan Saxon cemetery at Wally Corner, Berinsfield, 1974, by the Oxford Archaeological Unit.*

# The Earliest Evidence

## Jean Cook

Man first appeared in Britain during the Ice Age, reaching the Thames Valley approximately 400,000 years ago. The period that followed is known as the Old Stone Age or Palaeolithic. Tools were made of pebble or flint, worked by hand by a process of flaking. Flakes, removed by striking with a stone or antler hammer, were used as scrapers for skins and wood and for cutting meat, and the heavy cores left behind after the flakes had been removed were used as choppers. Flint-flaking is not an easy business and a large number of waste flakes would have been produced for each successfully completed tool. Worked flint is frequently the only evidence to suggest the presence of Palaeolithic man and distinguishing between man-made flakes and those produced by natural causes needs considerable expertise. A later development in this period was the hand-axe, an all-purpose tool which could be used for hunting, skinning, cutting and other jobs. Often these axes were beautifully shaped and finished, indicating a high degree of craftsmanship. Palaeolithic man had no permanent settlements and lived a nomadic life as a hunter-gatherer, searching for food. Evidence from bones preserved in the Dorchester gravel deposits suggests that the local animals living at that time included mammoth, woolly rhinoceros, horse, cave bear, cave lion and arctic fox.

After the retreat of the last ice sheets, Britain was left as a cold and marshy area, still joined to mainland Europe. Gradually changes in the sea level resulted in Britain becoming an island. About 6500 BC two other major factors slowly brought about a very different landscape. The climate became appreciably warmer, and the island was colonised by trees until there was an almost complete cover of alder, elm, lime and oak. This period is known as the Middle Stone Age or Mesolithic.

During this period the hunter-gatherer way of life persisted and Mesolithic man was regularly on the move in search of food. Tools were made of bone and flint, the flint often being worked into microliths — small, regular-shaped pieces set into wooden shafts to make knives, barbed spears and arrowheads. It is these microliths, in particular, which provide the evidence for the existence of Mesolithic man. Recent fieldwork in the Upper Thames Valley has indicated that it may be possible to identify, from groups of microliths, areas of concentrated domestic activity as distinct from a broad scatter over a wider area.

The Neolithic or New Stone Age marked a gradual change from the hunter-gatherer way of life to that of the earliest farmers. The idea of deliberately cultivating plants and domesticating animals rather than relying on haphazard naturally-occurring supplies meant that other changes could follow as a consequence. Man could begin to order his own environment. From about 4000BC in Britain Neolithic farmers began to clear away the forests to provide land for growing food. Crops included two kinds of wheat — emmer and einkorn — and barley. Animals which became domesticated during this period included cattle, pigs and sheep, though they would have looked very different from their modern successors. Neolithic man continued to hunt wild animals in uncleared forest areas as can be seen by the distribution of flint arrowheads. Considerable supplies of natural food would also have been available.

*Finely flaked Acheulian hand-axe from a gravel pit at Berinsfield. Over 200 Palaeolithic flint artefacts, as well as a number made from quartzite pebbles, have come from pits in this area.*

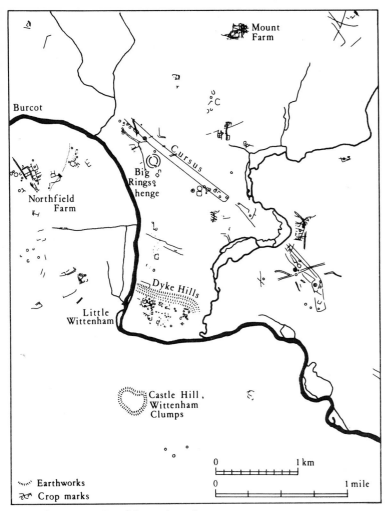

Earthworks
Crop marks

## Dorchester : Prehistoric sites

As they became more adept at controlling their food sources, Neolithic farmers were able to form more permanent communities. In any case some of the work, like woodland clearance, harvesting and looking after flocks, would almost certainly have needed co-operative effort. Another result of a more settled way of life was the development of new skills such as making polished stone axes and, most important of all from the archaeologist's point of view, the manufacture of pottery. Previously man had made carrying and storing utensils from wood, leather and in the form of woven baskets, but these objects soon decay, and only in exceptional circumstances, such as in waterlogged conditions, do they survive until today. Pottery on the other hand has a much longer lifespan,

and can survive intact over thousands of years. Neolithic pottery is often named after key sites where it was found, sometimes in a context which made it possible to suggest a date for the occupation of the site. When pottery of a similar kind is found elsewhere it is still called by the name for the key site and can be used, by analogy, to help date other sites. The earliest pottery is round-bottomed and rather baggy in shape, resembling the leather and basket vessels it replaced. One slightly later local style which is often decorated is called Abingdon ware, because it was found at a key site there. Ebbsfleet ware, from a site in Kent, also sometimes decorated, is another early style. Later in the Neolithic period the pottery shows a wider variety of decorative motifs, made by impressing the damp clay with finger nails, bits of twisted cord or small bird bones. Towards the end of the Neolithic period a characteristic pottery form was the beaker; this type of pot gave its name to the final stage of the Neolithic period. These pots often have more elaborate decoration, sometimes covering the whole of the body.

The Upper Thames Valley featured prominently during the Neolithic period, with a significant Neolithic presence at places such as Barrow Hills, Radley, Drayton, Burcot and Stanton Harcourt as well as Dorchester. Evidence does not come from domestic houses which rarely survive from this period; indeed Neolithic farmers were probably nomadic, at least for part of the time. In the case of Dorchester it comes instead from a large ceremonial complex to the north-west of the town. The Big Rings monument, one of the largest elements in the complex, was discovered by accident from the air by the RAF in 1927. At the same time other elements were noted and these were photographed by Major Allen in 1933. When the area was threatened by gravel extraction after the war a series of rescue excavations was carried out between 1946 and 1951 (Atkinson 1951). As a result Dorchester is known as one of the classic Neolithic sites in Britain. More recently, in 1981, work was carried out on part of the complex in advance of the building of the Dorchester by-pass. Most of the area is now

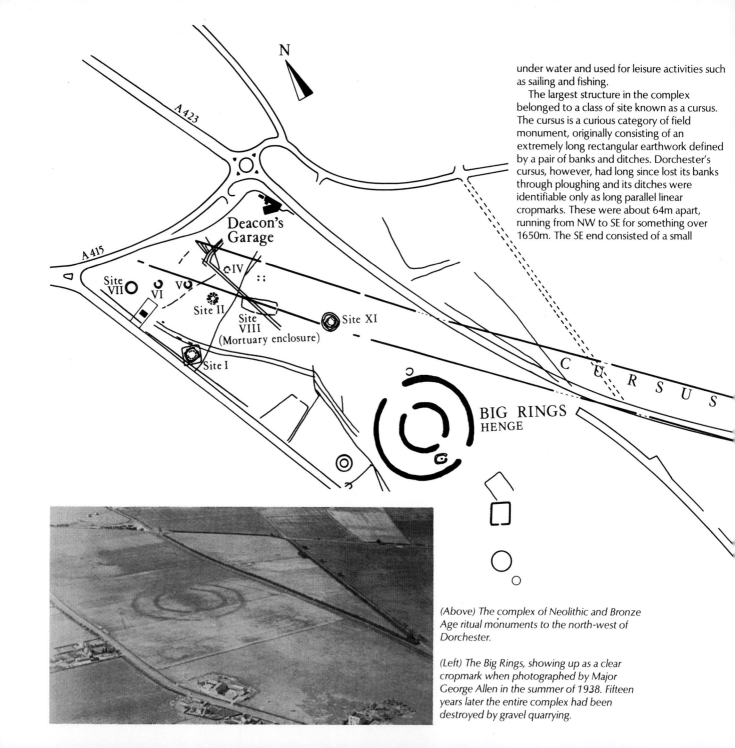

under water and used for leisure activities such as sailing and fishing.

The largest structure in the complex belonged to a class of site known as a cursus. The cursus is a curious category of field monument, originally consisting of an extremely long rectangular earthwork defined by a pair of banks and ditches. Dorchester's cursus, however, had long since lost its banks through ploughing and its ditches were identifiable only as long parallel linear cropmarks. These were about 64m apart, running from NW to SE for something over 1650m. The SE end consisted of a small

*(Above) The complex of Neolithic and Bronze Age ritual monuments to the north-west of Dorchester.*

*(Left) The Big Rings, showing up as a clear cropmark when photographed by Major George Allen in the summer of 1938. Fifteen years later the entire complex had been destroyed by gravel quarrying.*

D-shaped enclosure, bounded by a shallow ditch. During the earlier excavations fragmentary human remains were found in a pit within the enclosure; these have been dated to about 3,000 BC by radio-carbon analysis. This enclosure was again examined in 1981, when it was confirmed that the shallow ditch around the monument was interrupted by a central entrance on the SE side. The southeastern terminal ditch respected a small prehistoric monument which has been dated to approximately 2,000 BC by carbon 14 analysis. It is possible, however, that the cursus may not all have been built at the same time,

but that the D-shaped enclosure pre-dates the rest of the structure. Certainly the rest of the cursus was much more substantial. It is dated by a lozenge-shaped arrowhead found in the base of one of the ditches and by pieces of Ebbsfleet ware found in the upper ditch filling. The function of this monument is unknown but it may have had some ceremonial, possibly religious, significance. Several other examples have been identified elsewhere in the country; one is not far away, at Drayton, and another, still with surviving earthworks, lies close to Stonehenge.

Site VIII, excavated in 1948, was a

monument known as a mortuary enclosure. Sometimes such structures take the form of long barrows, but this one was a rectangular enclosure bounded on all four sides by a ditch with an internal bank. There were narrow entrance gaps on the two longer sides and a wider entrance in the centre of the shorter southern side. It is dated by the substantial sherds of Ebbsfleet ware which were found in the upper filling of the ditch; part of a human jaw from within the enclosure helps to confirm the mortuary function.

Site XI, excavated in 1949, consisted of three more or less concentric ditches, of different dates, enclosing an incomplete ring of 14 pits. The middle ditch seems to have surrounded an oval barrow or enclosure and to have then been converted to a circular plan. Some of the pits contained animal bones, one contained an antler pick and one contained a complete human cremation, but there were no accompanying grave goods.

Both these sites were in existence before the cursus was built. This is shown by the fact that the southernmost ditch of the cursus cuts through site VIII and abuts site XI. These two earlier sites seem to share the same alignment, but once the cursus was constructed it set a new alignment which may have been of significance until the end of the 3rd millenium BC. Three monuments built after the construction of the cursus were located inside it, two of them being along the central axis, and two others were just outside the southernmost ditch of the cursus but shared the same general alignment.

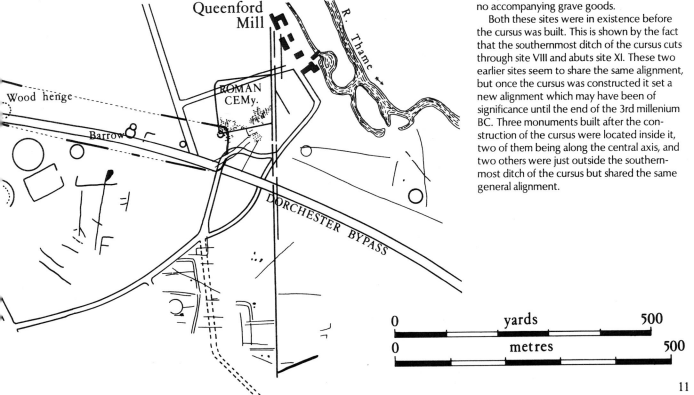

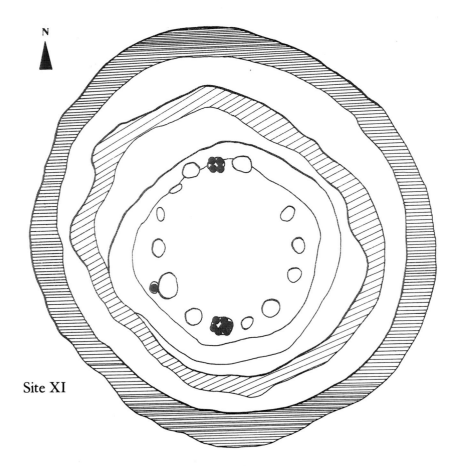

N

Site XI

*Plans of some of the sites excavated by Professor R. J. C. Atkinson prior to their destruction by gravel quarrying.*

0    metres    10

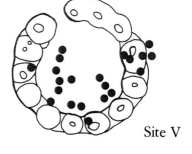

Site IV

Site V

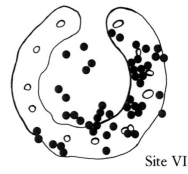

Site VI

Sites IV, V and VI, which were also excavated in 1949, have a similar overall plan and all of them contained a number of cremation deposits suggesting that amongst other things they acted as cemeteries. All three sites had a circular plan and consisted of an outer bank, to define the central area, and an inner ditch, the purpose of which seems to have been to provide earth for the bank. In Site IV the ditch was made up of eight oval pits, enclosing an area about six metres in diameter. There was a broad entrance gap on the south east side. Inside the enclosed area there were 25 deposits of cremated bones. An arrowhead was found with one of the cremations. Site V was very similar in construction, except that the entrance gap was on the north-western side, and contained 21 cremation deposits. No grave goods were found. Site VI again had a similar plan with the entrance gap to the north. There were 49 cremation deposits, one accompanied by a flint fabricator, an arrowhead and burnt flint flakes.

Site 1 was excavated in 1946 and consisted of a small square ditch, enclosing another more or less circular ditch with an internal bank. Inside this ditch were 13 holes, forming a ring with an entrance gap on the western side. There were no entrances in the surrounding ditches. A crouched burial was found within the entrance to the ring of holes but there were no accompanying grave goods. Four cremations were found, two accompanied by fragmentary bone pins, in or beside four of the central holes. At a later stage in the Neolithic period parts of the ditch may have been enlarged to make temporary shelters: it is not clear to which period of use the cremations belong.

Site II, also excavated in 1946, consisted of a causewayed (interrupted) ring ditch which was enlarged on two occasions. The third ditch had an internal bank in which were 19 cremation deposits. Two more cremations were found at the centre of the enclosed area. There was no evidence for any entrance gap. Bone pins were found with four of the cremations as were flint fragments. In addition, antlers and other flint fragments were found, as well as pieces of pottery.

In 1981 a small semi-circular enclosure ditch was excavated within the SE terminal of the cursus. Though sited off-centre the ditch shared the same alignment as the cursus. An antler (dated to c 2000 BC) was found close to the bottom of the ditch. After the ditch had virtually filled up with silt the surviving low central mound was used for cremation deposits, one of them associated with a heavily burnt flint blade.

Most of the sites in this group seem to have been built later than the cursus, and although it is not easy to see how they relate to each other it seems likely that some of them were in use at the same time. It is clear, however, that many of them were used as sites for the deposit of cremated bones. The weights of the individual bone deposits recorded by Professor Atkinson showed that something like half of the volume of bones of each cremation were gathered up from the funeral pyre. The bones were then deposited in a small pit in the ground, perhaps in some kind of bag. Few grave goods were buried with the bones.

Atkinson made some attempt to estimate the population from the cemetery evidence. He suggested that each of the burial grounds was for no more than one or two families and that they may have been used for a generation or so. The total population at any one time he reckoned as being around 40. Although such

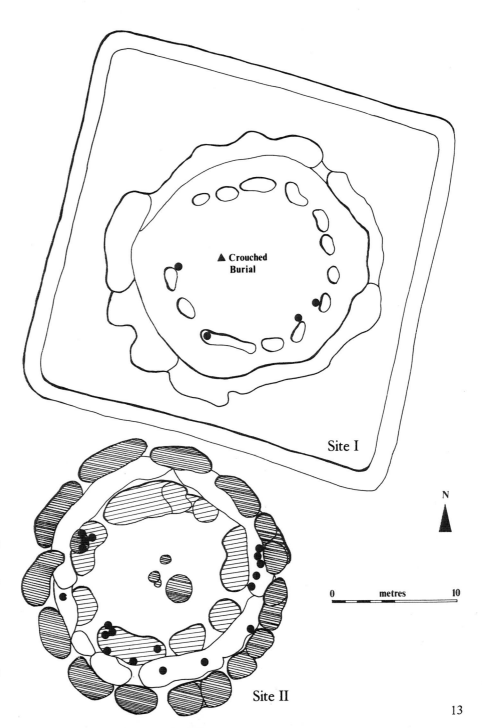

Site I

Site II

N

0     metres     10

13

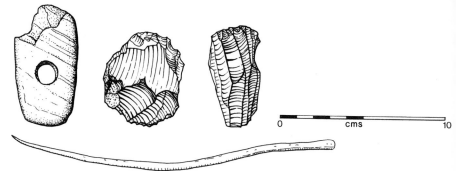

*(Right) Neolithic finds excavated at Dorchester in 1951: macehead of greenish/grey sandstone, flint flake, flint core and bone pin (Ashmolean Museum).*

*(Below) Beaker, with bands of incised and impressed decoration, together with associated finds — a wristguard of polished greenstone and two bronze daggers — excavated by Professor Atkinson in a barrow just to the north of the Big Rings (Ashmolean Museum).*

estimates have to be used with great caution and it is probable that a proportion of graves had already been ploughed out, such exercises are valuable.

Two more sites in this complex have been investigated. One was excavated in 1981 and was found to be a wood henge as opposed to a stone henge. It consisted of a ring of large pits enclosing an area some 18m in diameter. The site was situated along the central axis of the cursus, presumably influenced by the alignment. The pits, which varied in size, had each contained a wooden post, in three instances consisting of an entire trunk of an oak tree. All the posts were burnt *in situ*, presumably during some form of destruction ceremony.

The remaining site to be dealt with in this impressive complex is the Big Rings monument itself, one of the best known of the henge monuments. Henge is a term derived from Stonehenge (*henge* is an Old English word meaning, 'hanging'); most henge monuments, however, never had Stonehenge's hanging stones or lintels and consisted of a circle of standing stones or upright timbers, surrounded by a ditch and (usually external) bank. As with the rest of Dorchester's neolithic ritual complex, nothing remained above the ground surface. The banks and the ditches had been levelled through agricultural activity, possibly in the Iron Age. This particular henge probably dates from the middle of the second millennium BC and, interestingly enough, did not respect the alignment established by the cursus. The ditches, of which there were two, had

opposed entrances on the NNW and SSE. They were about 7.6m wide and about 1.8m deep with flat bottoms. Originally there seems to have been a broad low bank on the inner side of each ditch. The southern entrance incorporated an existing monument, consisting of a ring ditch which enclosed a large four-post setting and contained a cremation and a stone axe. Just outside the north entrance was a round barrow, containing a central oval burial pit which produced a crouched inhumation, together with a well-preserved beaker, two small copper or bronze knives and a rectangular wrist-guard of greenstone. The Big Rings ditches themselves contained pottery belonging to the middle or late Beaker period. Although the area within the ditches was trenched there was no evidence of internal timber structures.

The widespread use of bronze for making the finer ornaments, tools and weapons marked the start of the Bronze Age. It is now recognized that there was a considerable overlap between the Neolithic and Bronze Ages, and that the Neolithic way of life was still followed by metal users. Little is known about the pattern of land use in this period but it seems that settlement may have moved onto the sandier soils and that seasonal grazing may have been introduced. There is some evidence on the chalk Downs of carefully laid out field systems which may well have existed on the gravels as well. The absence of field ditches in the vicinity of the cursus and the henges, however, probably meant that the earlier monuments continued to be venerated in the Bronze Age.

14

0        cms       15

*(Left) Late Bronze Age shield, discovered in the Thames near Clifton Lock, near Dorchester, in 1980 (Ashmolean Museum).*

*(Below) Shield of sheet bronze with raised bosses, found in the Thames near Day's Lock in 1836 (British Museum).*

the dead. Instead rich metal work seems to have been deposited in rivers. One example is the bronze shield, found in October 1836 in the river Thames about a mile to the west of Dorchester, midway between Little Wittenham Bridge and the weir at Day's Lock. About 36cm in diameter, it is decorated with two circles of small raised bosses, with a larger raised area in the centre. Another is the splendid bronze shield, found in 1980, in the Thames to the north of Long Wittenham village, in the old course of the river near its junction with the Clifton Cut at Clifton Lock. This outstanding find can be seen in the Ashmolean Museum.

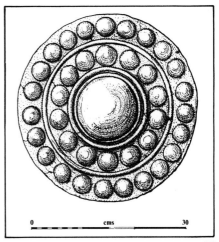

0       cms       30

Excavations in 1979 at Mount Farm, Berinsfield, which lies a little over one kilometre to the north, provided evidence of Neolithic and Bronze Age activity. In particular it revealed the presence of two pairs of small ditches, apparently forming trackways at the corner of a more extensive field system. Most of the evidence for the Bronze Age comes from graves. Round barrows, now frequently represented in the form of ploughed out 'ring ditches', are characteristic of the earlier part of the period and, in the Upper Thames Valley, seem to date from between 2,000 — 1100 BC. In the Dorchester area there were large groups of ring ditches close to the Big Rings henge monument.

Early in the first millennium BC the pattern of life seems to have changed. The earlier monuments were no longer in use and some were ploughed out. Pottery shapes changed, sometimes copying imported metal vessels, and grave goods were no longer buried with

# Before the Roman Conquest

**Jean Cook**

In Britain, the period between the Bronze Age and the Roman occupation is called the Iron Age; it began around 700 BC when iron working first appears in the archaeological record. By the end of the Bronze Age large ritual and burial monuments have gone out of fashion. However, unlike the preceding Bronze Age, the steadily increasing population has left behind a rich legacy of settlement remains and associated field boundaries. The remains around Dorchester are generally well preserved and represent one of the best examples of a late prehistoric landscape in the country.

For much of the Iron Age the dominant feature of the Dorchester scene would have been the hillfort on Castle Hill, Wittenham Clumps. As tribal groupings developed during the Iron Age, territorial boundaries became important and the River Thames provided a natural boundary. Dorchester lay on the boundary between three main tribal groups — to the north-west, occupying the Upper Thames Valley and the Cotswolds, were the Dobunni; to the north-east, in the Chiltern area, were the Catuvellauni; while to the south were the Atrebates, occupying the Middle Thames valley and the chalklands of central Southern England. The focus of attention in Dorchester shifted to the Iron Age hillfort on one of the low hills to the south of the river. The hillfort on Wittenham Clumps covers approximately 4 hectares (c. 10 acres) and comprises a single ditch and rampart. It commands superb views northwards up the Thames valley and to the south and west across the Vale of White Horse to the Berkshire Downs, where a series of similar hillforts follows the line of an ancient route — the Ridgeway. The fort has never been excavated, although frequent past ploughings have produced Iron Age and early Saxon sherds as well as Romano-British pottery.

However, to the south of the hillfort, in what is now a car park, a well-stratified Iron Age settlement site was found. It seems probable on the basis of other excavated sites that the fort was permanently occupied. It would have developed as a regional administrative and political centre, with specialist craftsmen and traders, and would have performed some of the same functions as a medieval market town.

Not much is known about early Iron Age settlements in the surrounding countryside; essentially the evidence comes from complexes of pits, which may originally have provided storage and were eventually used mainly for rubbish disposal. By contrast, for the middle Iron Age, it is now possible to identify a variety of settlement types, ranging from small short-lived farmsteads to more permanent sites, with surrounding ditches enclosing round huts, whose walls were made up of wooden uprights with wattle fillings.

During the late Iron Age, about the time of Christ, the focus of settlement again shifted. This time it moved back across the Thames, to the loop of the river south of the modern village, to a considerable site known as the Dyke Hills. This great enclosure, known to archaeologists as an *oppidum*, covered 46 hectares (c. 114 acres) and was defended by a massive double bank and ditch to the north and to the east. The southern and western boundaries have all but disappeared but can be traced in lines of modern field boundaries beyond which the Thames forms a natural boundary. The interior is apparently empty, but cropmarks reveal that it is full of enclosures, pits and circular houses aligned along a regular pattern of internal roads. Although there has been no scientific excavation within Dyke Hills, ploughing of the site has produced one of the densest concentrations of Iron Age coins in Britain.

*(Right, upper) The hillfort on Wittenham Clumps, photographed by Major George Allen in 1933.*

*(Right, lower) The fortifications at Dyke Hills and the complex of cropmarks which they enclose. Ditches, trackways, enclosed fields and hut-circles can be detected.*

*(Below) Coins of the Catuvellaunian kings Tasciovanus (c. 20 BC-AD 5) and Cunobelin (c. AD 5-AD 40), found near Dorchester and illustrated by Skelton in 'Antiquities of Oxfordshire', 1823.*

Dyke Hills is a site of major local, regional and national importance. It clearly played an important role in the life of the inhabitants of the Upper Thames Valley during the later Iron Age and up to the eve of the Roman Conquest of Britain. The Wittenham Clumps fort appears to have been abandoned or reduced in importance and some, if not all, of its functions were transferred across the river to the lowland site to enable a much larger settlement to be built and to reflect the growing status and importance of prehistoric Dorchester. The details of the role and function of Dyke Hills are unknown, but we can speculate that it was an important tribal centre carrying out all the administrative and political tasks associated with a prominent trading centre. We can also be sure that it was important commercially, both for the

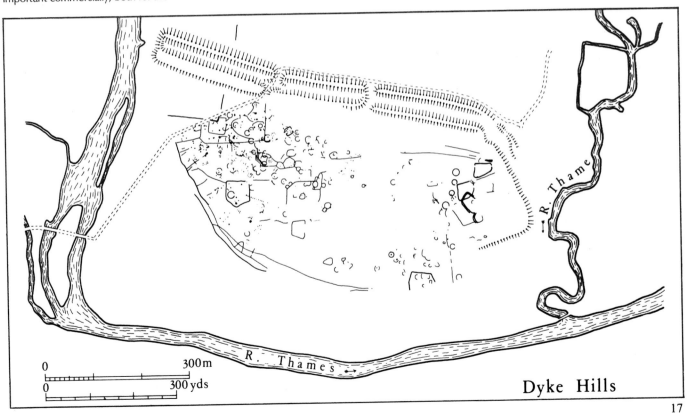

Dyke Hills

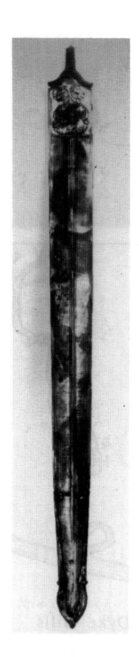

The splendid Celtic Iron Age sword in its bronze scabbard, found in a pond in Little Wittenham village in 1982. The scabbard mouth shows the curvilinear decoration characteristic of Celtic ornamental metalwork of the period (Ashmolean Museum).

manufacture and trade of a wide range of goods, some of them of a specialist nature. In other words if the hillfort on Wittenham Clumps can be compared to a medieval town, Dyke Hills was equivalent to a medieval city.

A section across the defences of Dyke Hills was excavated in 1870 by General Pitt-Rivers, then Colonel Lane-Fox, who was, at the time, the Honorary Secretary of the Ethnological Society of London. Concern was being expressed at national level because the owner of the land across which the dykes ran was allowing the left flank to be 'reduced for cultivation'. Indeed the Saturday Review of July 2, 1870, published an article on the Dorchester Dykes which gives us details of the measures being taken at the time to preserve the monument and has a depressingly modern ring to it:

> ... the fortress at Dorchester and the fortress on Sinodun (Castle Hill) are among the most speaking monuments of the earliest history of our island, and till lately they were among its most perfect monuments. But it is a grievous truth that while we are writing the dykes at Dorchester are being levelled. Hitherto the neighbouring ground has been grazed and the harmless sheep is no foe to history; but it has lately occurred to the owner of the ground that a few shillings more of yearly profit might be gained by turning pasture land into arable; and to such a sordid motive as this these precious antiquities are at this very moment being

sacrificed. At least a third of the dyke has been already lowered, and will gradually be utterly destroyed beneath the yearly passage of ruin's merciless plough share. Such wanton destruction naturally aroused the indignation of men of taste and knowledge, especially in the neighbouring University. A vigorous appeal to the owner to stay his hand was made by some of the most eminent Oxford residents, and an attempt was made to call public attention to the subject by describing the state of the case in various newspapers . . . .

There then follows a passage describing the confusion between Dorchester, Oxon and Dorchester, Dorset which, the writer says, 'has quenched public interest'. However the final paragraph is worth quoting in full:

Meanwhile the work of destruction is actually going on. The pickaxe and shovel were busily at work only a few days back; but meanwhile those who have the antiquities and the credit of the country at heart have been stirred up to more vigorous exertions. A memorial to the Home Office

*Dyke Hills, photographed in 1872, two years after Colonel Lane-Fox had drawn attention to the destructive agency of agriculture.*

19

was a few days back in the course of signature at Oxford, and it had received the names of many of the most eminent members of the University. The memorial prayed that any available means might be taken both to stop the hand of destruction in this particular case and to secure our national antiquities against such danger for the future. It is really frightful to think that so many of our most precious antiquities, both primeval and medieval, cromlechs, barrows, dykes, ruined churches, lie absolutely at the mercy of individual owners, who may happen to be liberal and intelligent, but who may also happen to be sordid and ignorant. The rights of property must have some limit. The law in many cases hinders a man from doing to his neighbours not only substantial, but even what might be called sentimental damage. He ought surely to be hindered in the same way from doing a damage to the whole nation by wiping out a portion of its history. A man may do as he wills with his own; but he should not be allowed so to do with his own as to destroy the right which every man has in the history and monuments of his country. We believe that the present Government is not unwilling to take some steps in the matter; and the part of the Dorchester dykes which has already fallen will not have fallen in vain if it leads to some measure for the permanent security of the daily threatened antiquities of our land.

Colonel Lane-Fox went to see the site for himself as a result of earlier articles in the press and persuaded the owner to stay his hand. A report of Lane-Fox's assessment of the site is published in a letter which he read to a special meeting of the Ethnological Society, held on June 21, 1870 and his plans and drawings are illustrated here.

*Colonel Lane-Fox's illustrations, published in the* **Journal** *of the Ethnological Society, 1870.*

Journ. Ethno. Soc. Vol. II. Pl. XXVI.

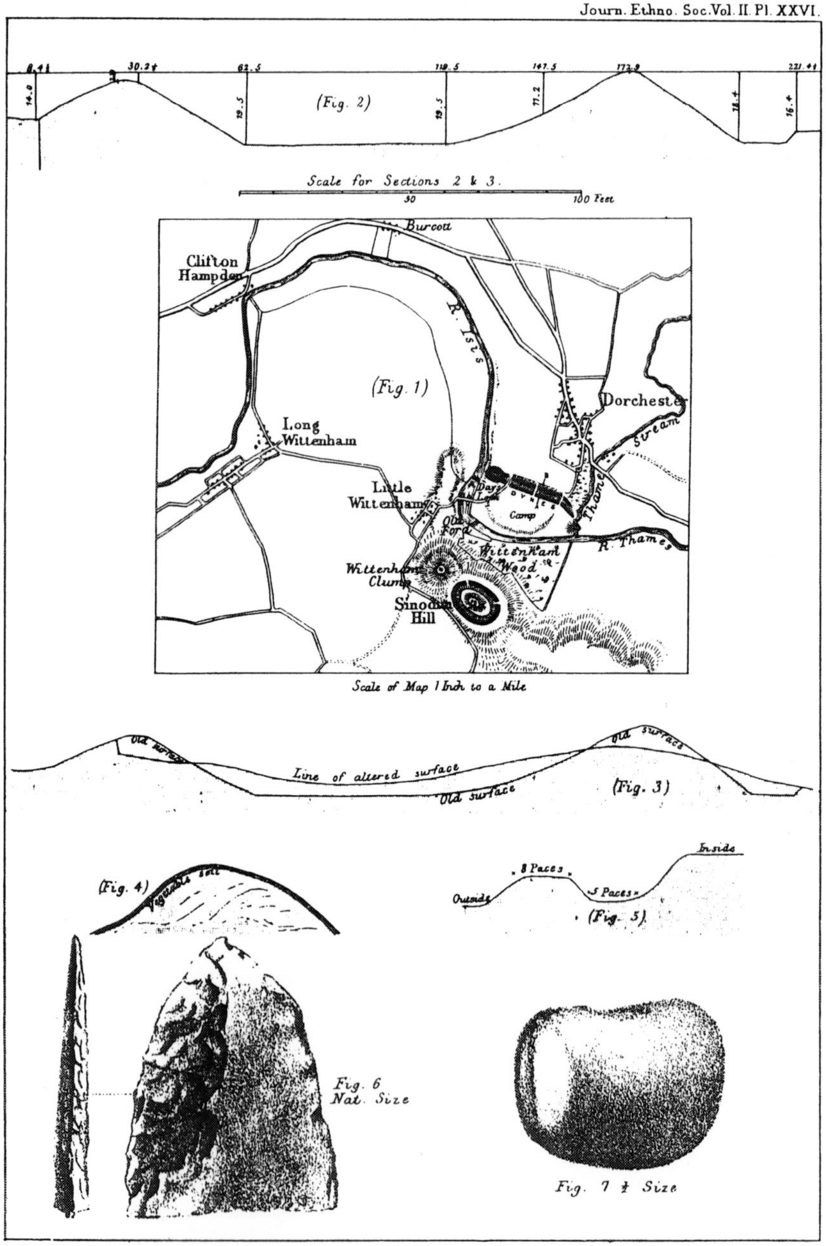

DORCHESTER DYKES & SINODUN CAMP.

# Roman Dorchester

**Trevor Rowley**

Dorchester's role as a place of considerable regional importance continued after the Roman conquest of Britain. Despite this obvious importance the Roman name of Dorchester is not recorded. The name 'Dorocina', marked on older Ordnance Survey maps, is wholly spurious — it was an invention of Charles Julius Bertram, an English teacher living in Copenhagen in the eighteenth century, who had sent to the eminent antiquary William Stukeley a text entitled *'De Situ Britainniae',* which purported to be a medieval history of Roman Britain. This forgery deceived generations of scholars before, like the Piltdown skull, it was finally exposed. The place name 'Dorcic' or 'Dorciccaestrae' is first mentioned by Bede in the 8th century. Although it has been suggested that the first element is British and derived from a root meaning 'bright' or 'splendid' place, this is not certain. The second element was commonly used by the Saxons to denote a place of Roman origin, generally with fortifications, and it has recently been speculated that it also signified some contemporary attribute, such as administrative status, which would have made these places suitable for the site of an early church.

Whatever name it was known by it is probable that Dorchester played a part in the military conquest of Britain in the mid-first century AD. Excavations and crop markings have located traces of a fort and wooden buildings of a type normally found in first century Roman forts. This fort lay a little to the north of the Dyke Hills complex, partly to the south of the later Roman walled town and partly under the Roman town. The siting of the fort to the north of the Dyke Hills, on the banks of the river Thame, initiated the final shift of the nucleus of settlement at Dorchester. The building of the fort was associated with the abandonment of the Dyke

Hills *oppidum,* but the identification of pre-Roman pottery and coins in the area of the modern village might suggest some shift of emphasis had already taken place by the time the Romans arrived. The siting of this fort was to influence the siting of the fortified town, which in its own turn influenced the location of the early Saxon cathedral and medieval abbey.

A coin of AD 78 seems to mark the end of the military phase in the town's history, as it was found in the remains of the demolished fort. Sometime afterwards a small civilian settlement was developed here and an irregular grid of streets laid out. The buildings associated with this phase of the town's history consisted largely of timber-framed buildings with clay floors. This type of building was constructed throughout the Roman town's history, and some, such as those found in excavations behind the Castle Inn, were of a relatively high standard, indicated by the presence of decorated wall plaster.

Other excavations within the town have revealed evidence of largely robbed out stone-based town houses, with tessellated (mosaic) floors and tiled roofs. A third century stone courtyard house was excavated in the north of the town and a small three-roomed rectangular building was constructed in the early fifth century in the south-west corner of the town. A Roman building lies beneath the abbey and a tessellated pavement was observed in a cellar on the west side of the High Street in the nineteenth century. Excavations seem to indicate that conditions within the town deteriorated during the fourth century. In the south-east section of the town rubbish pits were dug into former residential areas, while in the north-west a sequence of industrial kilns were erected on the site of the former courtyard house. Only two major phases of Roman occupation were found on

*Altar set up by Marcus Varius Severus in the late second or early third century, discovered in 1731 and since lost. Engraving from Richard Gough's edition of Camden's 'Britannia'.*

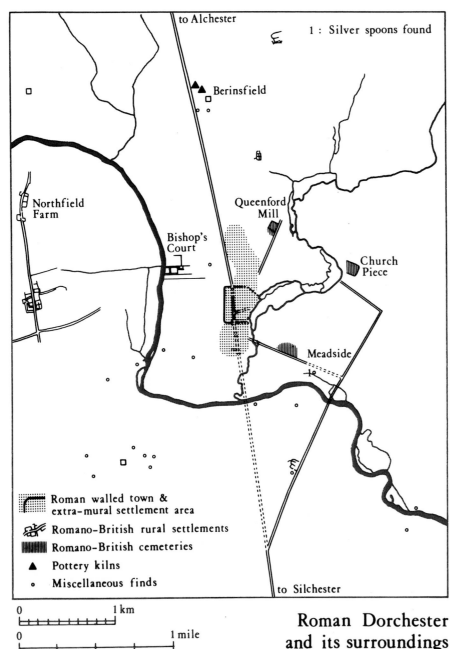

1 : Silver spoons found

to Alchester

Berinsfield

Northfield Farm

Queenford Mill

Bishop's Court

Church Piece

Meadside

**Roman walled town & extra-mural settlement area**

**Romano-British rural settlements**

**Romano-British cemeteries**

▲ **Pottery kilns**

◦ **Miscellaneous finds**

to Silchester

0         1 km

0         1 mile

## Roman Dorchester and its surroundings

the Beech House site, but elsewhere in the town there could well have been several more. In view of the town's apparent administrative importance it is perhaps surprising that no public buildings have been identified.

Dorchester's location on Thames valley gravels without any natural source of building stone has meant that generations of its inhabitants have dug for the Roman stone footings and in doing so disturbed the archaeological stratigraphy. Nevertheless numerous casual Roman finds from the town have been made. Among the more notable are the cremation burial from the garden of the vicarage, dated c.AD 200-250, which comprised a coarse red jar, three glass vessels and a lead cup, five silver spoons dug up in a gravel pit south-east of the town on the road to Benson, and an altar found in 1731. This was set up to Jupiter Optimus Maximus and the deity of the Emperor by Marcus Varius Severus, a *beneficiarius consularis,* and seems on epigraphical evidence to have been erected in the late second or early third century. A *beneficiarius consularis* was an official in the Roman army concerned with supplies and the collection of tolls and taxes. Such posts were normally established at cross-roads or near frontiers. His presence in Dorchester reflects its importance as a regional distribution centre of agricultural produce in the Roman period. "For such an officer, concerned with supplies, Dorchester with its rich surrounding cornlands afforded a centre conveniently placed for road and river transport". The town was clearly occupied in the early fifth century as demonstrated by the late Roman and early Saxon buildings, and it is one of a small group of sites that has produced a high percentage of coins of the late Roman emperor Theodosius (388-395) which are normally very scarce. This could well reflect the payment of late Roman or possibly mercenary soldiers stationed in the vicinity in order to protect the town.

The identification of certain types of military equipment from Dorchester and its surrounding area has been used to argue for the presence of such a protective force here in

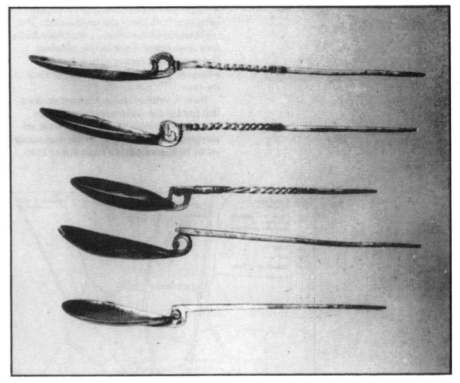

*(Right) Roman silver spoons, recovered from a gravel pit south-east of Dorchester in the early 1870s and now in the British Museum.*

*(Below) Roman glass vessels from the early third century cremation found in the Vicarage Garden in 1866 (Ashmolean Museum).*

the early fifth century. Additionally the coin evidence, together with ceramic and building evidence, shows a considerable amount of activity in and around the Roman town in the immediate post-Roman period. Dorchester-on-Thames has been identified as one of a small number of Roman towns where occupation and life style, perhaps in a modified Roman form, continued after the conventional end of Roman Britain in A.D. 410.

## The Roman Walls

Dorchester was one of the smallest walled towns in Roman Britain. Indeed the strength of the defences seems to be totally disproportionate to the small size of the enclosed area. The generally accepted extent of the walled area occupies only about 5.5 hectares (13.5 acres). Aston has suggested that the line of the eastern defences may also have incorporated the area later covered by the

Saxon cathedral and medieval Abbey. It is possible that the river Thame lay to the west of its present alignment and could have formed the eastern town boundary, in which case the defended area would have been somewhat larger. Excavations which took place at the Old Castle Inn site in 1972 should have located the line of the eastern defences, but there was no trace of ditch or rampart.

At the end of the second century an earth rampart was erected around the town and subsequently a wall was constructed in front of the rampart and the bank extended (c.A.D. 276-290). A V-shaped ditch contemporary with the earth rampart was succeeded by a flat-bottomed ditch 30m wide, which is believed to date from the fourth century. This would suggest that external towers were added in the mid fourth century, but it is possible that the second ditch was contemporary with the wall. Later, two small

V-sectioned ditches were cut in the upper filling over both lips of the original ditch. The construction of the defences must have had a fairly devastating effect on the suburban buildings, which appear to have been extensive, particularly on the southern side of the town.

There is some evidence from excavations that parts of the walls may have still been standing in the early Middle Ages. Walls are also mentioned in a charter to the Augustinian abbey by Eugenius III in a Papal Bull of 1146.

This charter, however, specifically mentions only that parts of a west wall were still standing. There is even some doubt if the walls referred to were Roman at all. The evidence from excavations by Rowley in 1972 and Chambers in 1982 is that they had been robbed out in the Saxon period in the north-western part of the town. Today signs of the flattened rampart and a broad shallow ditch can be seen in the allotment area representing the southern and south-western alignment of the Roman defences.

### The Extra-Mural Settlement

The Roman town at Dorchester is surrounded by cropmarks of all periods. A significant percentage of these belong to sites which contain evidence of Romano-British occupation. Many of them, such as the excavated sites at Bishop's Court, are agricultural in character; others, such as those to the immediate south of the town where numerous casual finds have been made, may be more properly designated as suburban. The population of Roman Dorchester would certainly not have been restricted to the walled area, and we have to envisage an area of occupation far larger than the few intra-mural hectares. Other cropmarks represent cemeteries or industrial sites such as the kilns of the Oxford Romano-British pottery industry which began to the north-east of the town and extend as far as Headington.

### Road System

The Roman road system which linked Dorchester to its neighbours probably had military origins, joining together those early forts, (of which Dorchester was one) which formed the framework on which the conquest of Britain was based. To the north the road ran through what is now Berinsfield and through the major areas of pottery manufacture to the east of Oxford, across Otmoor to Oxfordshire's other Roman walled town at Alchester. Subsequently this road proceeded northwards to join Watling Street (the A5) at Towcester.

The road system to the south of the town was somewhat more complicated. Logically

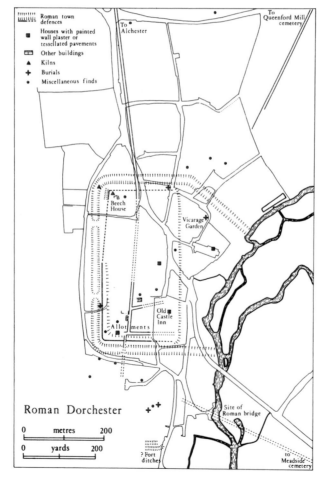

Roman Dorchester

the southern route should have crossed the Thames to the west of its confluence with the Thame and to the east of the Dyke Hills; that is immediately to the south of the Roman town. However, no trace of a ford has been found in the appropriate location and no trace of a Roman road has been found immediately to the south of the Thames. It is known that there was a crossing, a mile to the south-east of Dorchester, which has the appropriate place-name of 'Shillingford'. The road ran southwards from here to the now abandoned Roman town of Silchester (*Calleva Atrebatum*) in Hampshire. The enigma of Dorchester's southern Roman ford remains to be solved. Topographically the most acceptable location might be at the point just before the southerly flowing Thames does its abrupt turn eastwards. Here there are two islets, features often associated with the early river crossings. The alignment of another road running from the north-eastern corner of the town to a crossing of the Thame in the region of Stadhampton has been identified from aerial photographs and excavation. It was along this road that one of Dorchester's major Roman-British cemeteries was located in the region of Queenford Mill. Other possible alignments have been suggested to the east of the River Thame in the area of another of Dorchester's larger cemeteries.

Another important Roman road crossed the Thame below Meadside and ran southwards through Brightwell-cum-Sotwell and along Mackney Lane, apparently heading towards the Goring Gap. The Roman road system as a whole is, as yet, imperfectly understood, however, and further elements still await detection. Six kilometres to the east, in the parish of Chalgrove, are two fields called Stratford Meadow and Stratford Furrowlong, incorporating the place-name element *straet*, meaning a made road; they adjoin a long straight hedge which is followed by the parish boundary for 1.4 kilometres and points directly towards Dorchester. This may well be a fragment of a former link through to the Icknield Way and the Chilterns.

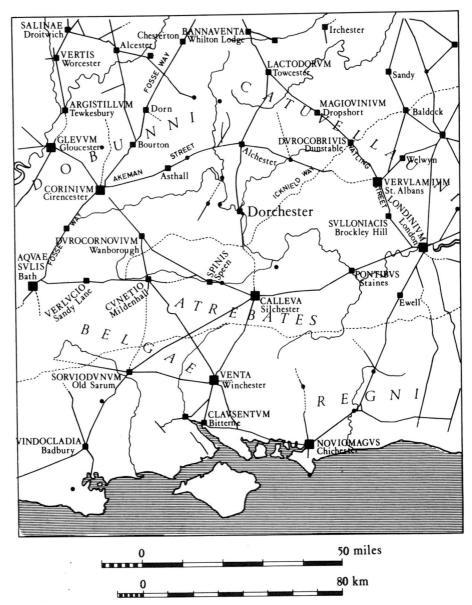

## ROMAN CENTRAL SOUTHERN BRITAIN

■ Coloniae, Cantonal Capitals & other large towns   ■ Small towns   ● Other settlements

25

### Cemeteries

Mineral working and redevelopment by other destructive agencies has meant that a considerable amount of evidence about Dorchester's Romano-British cemeteries has been brought to light. In the eighteenth century a Roman burial was found to the south-west of the town and this was accompanied by two pots and two glass vessels; there were also traces of other skeletons in the area. Roman burials have also been found immediately south of the town close to the large extra-mural settlement there. Although none of these burials has been accurately dated, it is probable that there is a substantial early Romano-British cemetery here. In 1874 and 1882 skeletons with associated Roman pottery were located during ditch digging in Meadowside Piece, alongside the probable line of the Roman road south-east of the town. This is close to the find-spot of the silver spoons. The only other evidence for earlier Roman burials is an early third century cremation south-east of the vicarage, to the east of the town. The location of a burial in this context might indicate that the line of the eastern defences did not include the site of the Abbey, as it was singularly rare for Roman burials to be found within the walled area.

The identification of the Queenford Mill and Church Piece cemeteries has clarified the cemetery problem for the later Roman period. Both seem to have been in use in the fourth century but not much earlier. If this is the case then we would expect the cemeteries of the first and second centuries to be closer to the town, near the main road. Queenford and Church Piece lie 700 and 1100m respectively from the town. Queenford has a straight track leading to it from the north-eastern corner of the town and the cemetery enclosure is laid out to the west at right angles to it. Church Piece is distant from Dorchester lying on the opposite bank of the Thame, a situation similar to *Verulamium's* (St. Albans) northern cemetery, across the river Ver. The present parish boundary is aligned on the Silchester road/river crossing and then runs at right angles, down Priests' Moor Lane, to a point adjacent to the southern side of the cemetery. The alignment of this parish boundary may well reflect an earlier Roman line. Cropmarks indicate a trackway running north from Priests' Moor Lane alongside the cemetery and another at the northern end curving down to the Thame. These may have provided access to the burial ground and we could expect that there would have been a river crossing in this area.

The best known late Roman burials around Dorchester are the Germanic graves from Dyke Hills and the Minchin Recreation Ground. There is no evidence for more extensive cemeteries in these areas, but the massive earthworks of Dyke Hills would have provided an obvious prominent feature in which to insert the graves of individuals belonging to a cultural minority in late Roman Dorchester.

The site at Queenford Mill was excavated in 1972 and again in 1981 and proved to be an extensive late Romano-British and sub-Roman cemetery. On the basis of this work we can assume that the total of burials within the enclosure was in excess of 2,000. The vast majority of the graves were aligned roughly west-east and a considerable number of the graves were aligned within discrete, possibly family, groups, indicating that they were marked. The complete absence of grave goods, the alignments, and a number of late fouth/early fifth-century carbon 14 dates all point to a late date for this cemetery, and its size suggests use over a long time, perhaps throughout the fourth and well into the early fifth century AD.

The other major cemetery to receive attention was at Church Piece. Although fieldwalking on the site produced first century pottery, most of the finds were of late Romano-British wares. Over the southern area of Church Piece a concentration of building debris, stone, plaster, tesserae and, particularly, red tile, indicated the presence of a Romano-British building. A faint rectangle with a central partition was also visible in the cropmarks in this area, and might represent the structure itself. In the south-east corner of the site it has been suggested above that a more complex tripartite building can be seen. In 1766 buildings were located in approximately this area of Boywere Furlong.

"In March and April Thos. Beisley and Willm. Wickens dug up some old Foundation Walls in Boywere Furlong by Prissmoor Lane in the Lower field of Warborough in the County of Oxford, which ground Platt measured by Edwd. Beaper, Clerk, and the North and South sides wall was 64 Feet long, being the longest that way. The East and West sides measured 60 foot 6 inches, in Length (or width) this being the Shortest Side. And there was also at the same time a Stone Coffin with Dry bones in and other Carcasses found in Church Piece, and Foundations of old walls, and a Small flower Pot found in the Coffin by order of Mr. Benjamin Bisley (or Beisley) was Buried again. These Memorials was Dug up when the Revd. Doctor Francis Randolph was Minister at Warborough, and Edward Beaper Parish Clerk at that time".

The "foundations of old walls" in Church Piece itself were not precisely located but confirm the results of modern field walking.

It is particularly interesting to find buildings in association with a cemetery. The tripartite plan of the major structure is familiar at a number of villas, notably, within Oxfordshire, at Ditchley. Whether this building functioned as a villa or was connected with the organization of the cemetery is still a matter for speculation.

Trial excavation showed that the wide cemetery ditch was in use in the late Roman period. It seems that although there is earlier occupation on the site, the principal features belong to the late third or fourth, and possibly fifth, centuries AD. It is not possible to say for how long the cemetery was in use, although the large number of burials would suggest some considerable time. The graves are in regular ranks, with little obvious disturbance and probably therefore had markers of some sort. The cemetery may have expanded beyond its first obviously crowded area into the southern enclosure, which seems still to have had room for a few more occupants when abandoned. The three ring-ditches may well pre-date the cemetery but it is feasible that they represent mausolea. One of the prime finds from this site was a plain Romano-British lead coffin, recovered when the area was being deep ploughed.

It seems likely that the two cemeteries at Queenford Mill and Church Piece contain most of the burials of the last century of Roman occupation in Dorchester. The Queenford cemetery enclosure (110x120m) covers 1.3 hectares (c.3.2 acres) and that at Church Piece (125x55m) 0.7 hectares (c.1.7 acres). If both cemeteries were fully utilized then there may be in the region of 3,000 burials over approximately 150 years. Although these figures are speculative, if they represent something approaching the total number of burials in late Roman Dorchester, then they indicate a local population of perhaps 600 people; a reasonable size for such a town with its suburbs.

The dating evidence suggests that both cemeteries were in use through the fourth and in the early fifth centuries. The burials are aligned as close to west-east as Dorchester Abbey itself. The excavated skeletons lay supine with their heads to the west and there was a complete absence of grave goods in both cemeteries. The fact that several hundred burials at both sites were so uniformly arranged does not necessarily demonstrate the Christianity of the deceased; their burials simply conform to a late Roman fashion. There is no positive evidence in the form of inscriptions, symbols or architecture to indicate the presence of Christianity in late Roman Dorchester, although the historical background of the period provides no major

*Bronze coin of the emperor Nerva (AD 96-98) found in excavations at Dorchester (about 3 times actual size).*

obstacle to such a belief. By the 380s Theodosius had established Christianity as the state religion and Dorchester, at a junction of routeways, was clearly open to new influences. In the light of Dorchester's subsequent history it is tempting to speculate what role the town might have played in the organization of late Roman Christianity in Britain. It seems highly likely that the Saxon cathedral lies under the present church, and probably outside the alignment of the eastern walls. Although there are a large number of early churches which sit within the walls of Roman towns, there are several that are situated just outside on the sites of Roman cemeteries. The church of St. Pancras and the Abbey of St. Augustine's in Canterbury lie on Christian inhumation cemeteries, the latter of which seems to have been pagan in origin, while the excavated Saxon church in the monastic graveyard of St. John's Abbey, Colchester, incorporated part of a Roman mausoleum in its fabric. It becomes tempting then to speculate on a similar origin for the church at Dorchester, particularly when one remembers the proximity of the cremation burial in the Vicarage garden and a tradition of a Roman building lying underneath the abbey. It is possible that the large amount of Roman material, accounting for well over a half of the 3m of stratigraphy recorded in the 1962 excavations on the north of the church, is not a reflection of the site lying within the occupied area enclosed by the defences, but of its being on top of a cemetery. Significantly 'Saxon' burials were also recorded from the excavation.

The Vicarage garden cremation was found 1.2m below the ground surface, also indicating a considerable build-up of soil. The possibility that a cemetery here became Christian in the late Roman period cannot be ruled out at this stage.

The idea that a Roman building lies under the abbey church is strengthened by its 'incorrect' orientation East-South-East to West-North-West, and also by the reference to the discovery of a Roman pavement, underneath which was burnt corn and bones, under the north-east chapel of the abbey (*Oxford Times* 4 June 1886).

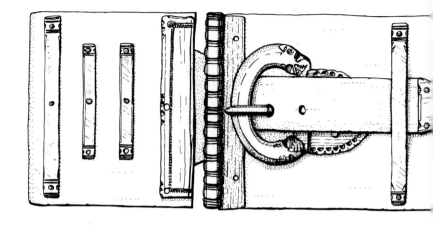

*Germanic mercenaries in Dorchester? Finds from nearby graves, including military belt fittings (above) and women's brooches of North German type (below) suggest that Germanic elements were present in Dorchester's population at the beginning of the fifth century, perhaps as part of the garrison of the town.*

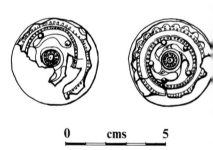

0    cms    5

In any case, Dorchester is just the kind of place where one would expect to find a 'capella memoriae', commemorating some now forgotten Romano-British martyr, of the sort recently discovered under the Saxon cathedral at Wells, where, incidentally, no Roman origin was previously suspected. Taking the statement in the 571 entry in the Anglo-Saxon Chronicle at face value, that is that the area remained in British control until the Battle of Bensington, it is quite possible that some memory, or even practice of Christianity survived at Dorchester well into the 6th century. Was the eventual choice of Dorchester as the diocesan centre of Anglo-Saxon Wessex in the early 7th century a reflection of a role performed two centuries earlier? The answers to this and related questions are not known......yet!

*(Right) Some of the 101 graves excavated at the pagan Saxon cemetery at Wally Corner, Berinsfield, in 1974.*

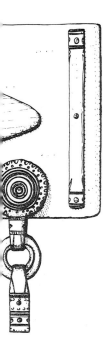

# Early Saxon Dorchester

**Jean Cook**

For the sake of convenience the six centuries from the end of Roman Britain to the Norman Conquest are called the Anglo-Saxon period. However, they were centuries of great ethnic, political and social upheaval, during which the basis of the medieval national state of England was being created. During this period for the first time the evidence discovered by the spade is seriously supplemented by the evidence of the written word. Although much is still speculation, for the first time we begin to learn the actual names of individuals and the actual dates of events. Despite the Roman interlude it is during this period that prehistory gives way to history.

As Roman Britain becomes England (and Wales) Dorchester plays an important and fascinating role within a kaleidoscopic drama of ever changing characters and events. From time to time during this period Dorchester appears to regain the ascendency in the Thames Valley it had enjoyed during the late Iron Age, but by 1066 it had irrevocably lost its regional importance to other, new centres, most notably Oxford.

By 410 AD Britain had ceased to be regarded as part of the Roman Empire. During the 4th century the country had been the target for a series of attacks by Picts, Scots and Saxons and reinforcements for the army in Britain had been sought from the continent. Sometimes support took the form of foreign mercenaries, often of Germanic origin. Some of these soldiers were possibly invited by the Romano-British inhabitants of Dorchester to defend them and appear to represent the vanguard of the Anglo-Saxon settlement. Although the native occupants of Dorchester may well have been Christian by this stage, the newcomers were most definitely pagan and buried their dead in a highly distinctive manner. This often involved the burial of semi-precious jewels or weapons alongside the corpse, which was sometimes dressed in fine clothing, occasionally making it possible to identify social status. Skeletal analysis also enables sex, age and certain illnesses to be identified.

In 1874 the burials of a man and a woman, accompanied by early Anglo-Saxon grave goods, were found in the Dyke Hills ramparts. The male burial produced a buckle, tubular-sided plate, metal strips and disc attachments, all of bronze, which have close parallels in material found on the continent along the military frontier-zone of northern Gaul and the Rhineland. Although no weapons were recorded from this Dorchester burial a note about the finds mentions that "much was thrown away by the men digging down the mound". The presence of the belt-fittings in itself does not prove that the owner was a Germanic mercenary, since they seem to have been standard equipment in the late Roman army, but the woman's grave, found close by, contained another military type buckle and two brooches, one a very early form of Germanic cruciform brooch and the other the back-plate of an applied brooch. Another female grave from Minchin Recreation Ground contained a pair of applied brooches and the back-plate of a third, all almost certainly of

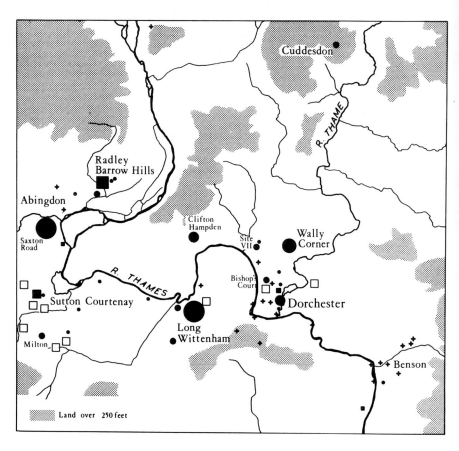

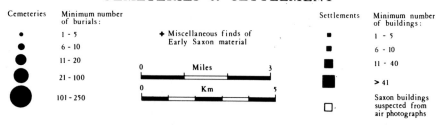

## DORCHESTER REGION : EARLY SAXON CEMETERIES & SETTLEMENT

| Cemeteries | Minimum number of burials : |
|---|---|
| • | 1 - 5 |
| ● | 6 - 10 |
| ● | 11 - 20 |
| ⬤ | 21 - 100 |
| ⬤ | 101 - 250 |

✦ Miscellaneous finds of Early Saxon material

| Settlements | Minimum number of buildings : |
|---|---|
| ▪ | 1 - 5 |
| ■ | 6 - 10 |
| ■ | 11 - 40 |
| ■ | > 41 |
| □ | Saxon buildings suspected from air photographs |

north German origin, a Roman bronze key and a collection of bracelets and rings. All these objects are on exhibition in the Anglo-Saxon gallery of the Ashmolean Museum. These three burials suggest the presence, very early in the 5th century, of Germanic people, possibly a mercenary soldier and certainly two women, in Dorchester. The man could have been a member of a garrison of *foederati* in the Roman town.

Evidence for the arrival in the Dorchester area of Saxons in larger numbers has come from archaeological excavation of cemeteries and settlement areas. Some instances of cremation have also been recorded, the burnt bones being buried in the ground in pots and sometimes with objects which may also have been burnt, but these are relatively infrequent.

There are several Saxon cemeteries in the area. Nine inhumations were found by Professor Atkinson in 1947 within the ditched area of a round barrow in the prehistoric complex to the north of the town (Site VII). These graves are likely to be of 6th century date; a male burial recorded in 1863 came from nearby and may have belonged to the same cemetery. At Bishop's Court, just to the north-west of Dorchester, three skeletons were found close to the garden wall of Bishop's Court House in 1857. Two more were recorded as being found during the digging of a drain through the yard. These were chance finds, but in 1958 a rescue excavation revealed ten inhumations found at the south-west corner of a 'tramline' cropmark, well known from aerial photographs. Only one was accompanied by grave goods, in the form of two iron knives which are now in the Ashmolean Museum.

The most recently excavated cemetery was found at Wally Corner, Berinsfield, a little to the north-north-east of Dorchester. The site was uncovered in 1974 as a result of gravel working and although the excavation was carried out as a rescue dig, and at speed, most of the cemetery was recovered. In all, 101 graves were excavated, with a total of 111 individuals, as some graves were multiple burials. Seven of the graves were lined or packed with limestone pieces of various sizes and two contained evidence of charred wood; one grave contained both limestone and charred wood. There were five cremations. Many of the graves contained grave goods. There were almost equal numbers of men and women among the adults. The women, particularly vulnerable during childbirth, seem to have died at a younger age than the men and in any case most people, of both sexes, died before they were forty-five. Weapons and jewellery date from the 5th to the 7th century and are characteristic of the Upper Thames Valley region in this period. The types of brooches present — saucer, disc, square-headed and equal-armed — suggest a strong Saxon tradition. No swords were found in any of the male graves but one, at least, of the female graves contained enough jewellery to suggest a lady of some status. She had a great square-headed brooch, two saucer brooches, a double string of amber beads and a shorter string of smaller glass beads, a bronze buckle and an iron knife. Fabric traces on the brooches indicate that she was wearing a woollen garment like a dress, with the saucer brooches functioning as fastenings on the shoulders, and an over-garment of linen, perhaps a cloak, fastened in the middle by the square-headed brooch. The beads hung in strings from between the saucer brooches.

The early Saxon settlers appear to have brought an unusual form of dwelling with them. These were sunken-featured huts, or *grubenhauser* as they are normally called. The depressions which were dug into the ground were relatively small, averaging 2.5 × 4 metres, and relatively shallow, being rarely deeper than 1 metre. They had wooden posts at either end supporting some kind of roof structure. The walls were probably filled in with wattle and the roof may well have been thatched. In some cases there is evidence that there was a wooden floor, covering a hollow area which could have been used for storage.

*One of the richest graves from Wally Corner; the woman was buried wearing a great square-headed brooch, a pair of large saucer brooches (one illustrated below), two strings of amber beads and a string of glass beads.*

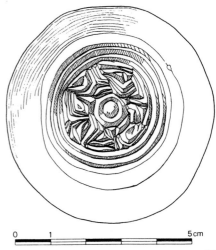

0    1                              5 cm

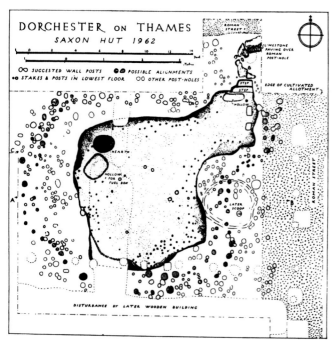

DORCHESTER ON THAMES
SAXON HUT 1962

○○ SUGGESTED WALL POSTS    ●○ POSSIBLE ALIGNMENTS
•○ STAKES & POSTS IN LOWEST FLOOR    ○○ OTHER POST-HOLES

DISTURBANCE BY LATER WOODEN BUILDING

In the north-western section of the town a sequence of Saxon buildings, dating from the 5th/6th century to the 9th century, were found. The earliest phase consisted of sunken-featured buildings followed by small rectangular timber-framed dwellings and finally dry-stone and cob buildings, roughly dated by a penny of King Burgred of Mercia of about 865 found under the latest wall. As already noted, the absence of good local building stone has meant that mud buildings have a long tradition in Dorchester, possibly lasting without interruption from prehistoric times to the present day.

*Plan of the irregularly shaped Saxon hut excavated in 1962; the reconstruction shows one possible interpretation of the house structure.*

*Fine bone hair comb (its teeth now broken) found in excavations at the Old Castle Inn site in 1972.*

The traces left in the ground of such buildings are normally only recognisable by changes in soil colour and can therefore be difficult to detect and excavate. However, evidence of sunken huts of 6th century date has been found on three sites within the area of the Roman walled town of Dorchester and also at Bishop's Court and to the north of Dyke Hills.

Not all Dorchester's Saxon buildings had sunken floors; regular rectangular buildings have also been found, both within and outside the town. During Frere's excavations in the allotment area he made an interesting discovery in the form of a sunken-featured dwelling of the 5th century aligned along a Roman road while not far away he located a 6th century rectangular building constructed over the surface of the road. This suggests that the earliest Saxon settlers used the internal street system but that it was fairly rapidly discarded. It is quite possible that other structures lie hidden under existing buildings or may have been destroyed by later developments.

Other evidence of Anglo-Saxon settlement comes from a number of chance isolated finds made in Dorchester. Unfortunately details of the sites were rarely recorded. One such find, now lost, was a gold and garnet pyramidal stud 'found by digging under a hedge', the closest parallel to which comes from Sutton Hoo in East Anglia. Two gold coins have also been found, a Saxon runic issue of 640-650 AD and a solidus of the Byzantine emperor Mauricius Tiberius, usually referred to as Maurice, of 582-602. The quality of these few finds suggests that the late 6th-early 7th-century Dorchester community might have been wealthy, possibly even princely, to judge from the stud.

*Drawing, in the Minute Book of the Society of Antiquaries, of the gold and garnet stud found at Dorchester about 1776.*

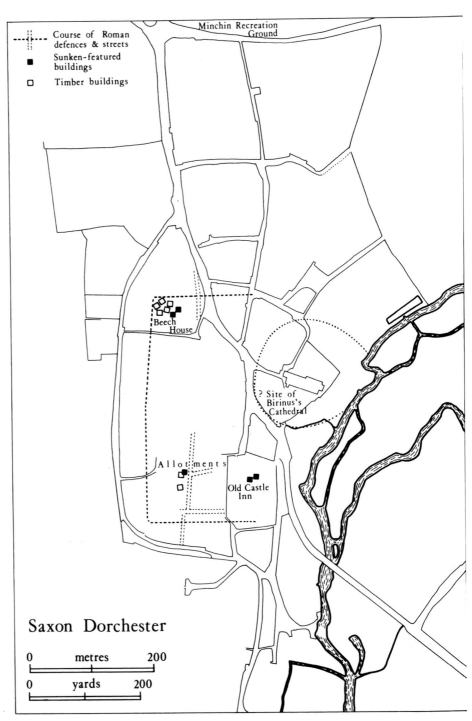

Course of Roman defences & streets

Sunken-featured buildings

Timber buildings

Minchin Recreation Ground

Beech House

? Site of Birinus's Cathedral

Allotments

Old Castle Inn

## Saxon Dorchester

| 0 | metres | 200 |

| 0 | yards | 200 |

PROTEGE : BIRINE : QV

SINE : FINE : PAR : RAST

*Inscription invoking Birinus, on the rim of the tenor bell of Dorchester Abbey, mid-fourteenth century.*

By this time Oxfordshire had become part of the kingdom of Wessex and Dorchester was clearly a focal centre in the Upper Thames region. It was conveniently situated on roads and rivers in the middle of an area of dense Anglo-Saxon settlement. In AD 635 a very important event took place in the town, which Bede records in his Ecclesiastical History, (Book III.7.) Birinus was sent to Britain by Pope Honorius I as a missionary to continue the conversion of the Anglo-Saxons to Christianity. He was consecrated bishop for this task at Genoa by Asterius, Archbishop of Milan. Birinus' original plan was to penetrate well into the interior of the country where no teacher had been before. However, "on arriving in Britain and first coming to the nation of the Gewisse (West Saxons), where he found all to be confirmed pagans, he thought it more useful to preach the word there, rather than to go further looking for people to whom he should preach".

It so happened that King Oswald of Northumbria, who had already been converted to Christianity by Celtic Christians in Scotland, wanted to marry the daughter of Cynegils, King of the Gewisse. Oswald therefore came to Dorchester to visit Cynegils, who had meanwhile been receiving instruction in the Christian faith from Birinus, and stood sponsor for him at his baptism by the bishop in AD 635. The two kings then granted land to Birinus in Dorchester for the establishment of his episcopal see and cathedral church. Birinus

thus became the first bishop of the West Saxons.

There is an interesting account in Richard Gough's edition of Camden's *Britannia*, (1806), Vol. II, of the finding in 1736, of "a small ring of the purest gold, inscribed within the year of Birinus' consecration 636; in it was set a cornelian . . . It was supposed a mitre on an altar or pillar, by the late Mr. Bilson, a Proctor of the University Court and rector of St. Clements, Oxford, to whom the ring was given and who, after refusing 20 guineas for it, left it to Mr. Applegarth, Schoolmaster, next door to the White Hart and he to Mr. Day, whose brother a wheeler now possesses it (1781)". This ring is said to have been found 'in a garden behind the church': its present whereabouts are unknown and it is not possible, without seeing it, to comment either on its date or on whether it actually records the beginning of Birinus' ministry.

Not much is known about Birinus, but Bede makes it clear that he built and dedicated churches and converted many people to Christianity by his teaching. He died about AD 650 and was buried in Dorchester. His relics were moved to Winchester around 690 by Bishop Hedda, who was at that time bishop of Winchester, and they remained there into the Middle Ages, being moved to new shrines in 980, by Bishop Ethelwold, and again in 1150 by Henri de Blois. By the early 14th century a shrine in memory of Birinus had been built at Dorchester and his feast — December 3 —

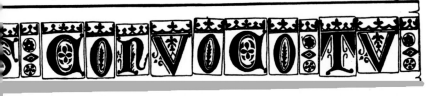

was added to the Roman martyrology in the late sixteenth century. The shrine presently to be seen in Dorchester Abbey is a modern reconstruction of the earlier monument. Other commemorations of St. Birinus are in stained glass windows in the Abbey and in the Roman Catholic church of St. Birinus; an inscription on the rim of the mid-fourteenth century tenor bell in the Abbey reads:
*Protege Birine quos convoco tu sine fine Raf Rastlwold.* ("Do thou, Birinus, protect for ever those whom I summon." Ralph Rastlwold (d. 1383) the donor of the bell, held the manor of Crowmarsh Gifford, six km south-east of Dorchester, and also lands at Hurst near Wokingham, where the bell was cast). Birinus is also amongst the figures carved on the great altar-screen in Winchester cathedral.

The events of the conversion of the King and the establishment of the West Saxon see suggest that in AD 635 Cynegils had a centre of power in Dorchester and that he may well have had a palace in the area. So far there is no archaeological evidence as to where this might have been though Bishop's Court has been suggested as a possible site. Nor do we know where Birinus' church was, though evidence from the siting of the Old Minster at Winchester suggests that the later Abbey Church could well mark the site of the first cathedral. The choice of Dorchester as the seat of the first Bishop's see has intrigued and tantalised scholars for generations. What particular attributes did this small sub-Roman town have to warrant such a distinction?

Both political and strategic factors may have played an important part in the choice of Dorchester as the ecclesiastical and administrative centre of Wessex in the early 7th century. The expansion of Wessex had been marked, according to the Chronicle, by battles at Salisbury in 552, Barbury Castle (Wilts) in 556, and Dyrham, which led to the capture of Cirencester, Gloucester and Bath in 577. In 584 King Ceawlin fought at 'Fethan leag', near Stoke Lyne (Oxon), and this may have marked the northernmost boundary of the kingdom. In any event it is clear that Dorchester was on the northern edge of a kingdom largely restricted to the south of the Thames and this location may make it seem an odd choice for the establishment of the West Saxon bishopric.

One reason for the selection of Dorchester may have been the wish on Cynegils' part to strengthen further his ties with King Oswald, who was at the time overlord of all the Anglo-Saxon kingdoms. Another is that it may have been a strategic move with a view to the conversion of the kingdom of Mercia immediately to the north. A third reason could have been precisely that Dorchester *was* on the northernmost limit of the kingdom and therefore well situated on the frontier of an area which, as we shall see, was disputed territory between Wessex and Mercia from the 7th to the 9th centuries.

It is perhaps more difficult to ascertain why Dorchester rather than any other place in the northern part of Wessex was chosen to be Birinus' seat, even if, as has been suggested and the Anglo-Saxon Chronicle implies, Cynegils was king of only the Northern part. It may have been felt that its former status as Roman 'civitas' gave it a certain dignity and this would be in accordance with Pope Gregory's instructions to the early missionaries that they should establish themselves in former Roman towns. This does not, of course, mean that the town was functioning in any sense as an 'urban place' by this date, although the discovery of the elaborately decorated pyramidal stud and the dense concentration of settlement in the area makes it possible that it was already a royal centre.

Alternatively it might be suggested that the royal centre was not at Dorchester itself, but at nearby Cuddesdon, where princely burial finds have also been recorded, or at Bensington (Benson). Curiously it is Bensington rather than Dorchester which is recorded in the Anglo-Saxon Chronicle for 571 as being taken by the Saxons (along with Limbury, Aylesbury and Eynsham), after the Battle of 'Biedcanford'. Perhaps, then, it was Benson which was the centre of political/royal power at this time and Dorchester had some other function. Certainly Benson is recorded as a 'villa regalis' by 887.

It may simply be that we should not expect to find physical traces of continuity of settlement for the two centuries after the end

*Two-headed bronze ornament, of uncertain use and late Saxon date, found near Bishop's Court and adopted as the emblem of the Oxford Archaeological Unit.*

of Roman rule within or immediately outside the walled area of Dorchester. If we apply what may be termed the 'Winchester model' to Dorchester, the town would have remained only of importance for the ruling element (possibly the descendants of the 'foederati') and would have been ringed by surrounding agricultural settlements and cemeteries. To compare the situation further with Winchester the Saxon settlement at nearby King's Worthy had developed by c.500 and a similar situation may have occurred at Canterbury. Perhaps at Dorchester, then, we should be thinking of a more dispersed settlement pattern in the sub-Roman period.

In any event, when Cynegils died his son, Cenwalh, succeeded him. He had not been baptised with his father and, although originally married to the sister of Penda, King of the Mercians, he took another wife. Presumably partly in revenge Penda attacked him and drove him out of Wessex into exile in the East Anglian kingdom, where he was converted. On being restored to his own kingdom again he appointed Agilbert, a Gaulish bishop, to the see at Dorchester. However king and bishop did not get on well together, because, according to Bede, the king, who only spoke his native Saxon, grew tired of his Bishop's 'outlandish speech'. In consequence Cenwalh divided the bishopric, without consulting Agilbert, and created a new see in Winchester in the 660s. He had already built a church there in AD 648, which Birinus may have dedicated towards the end of his life. The foundations of this church of SS Peter and Paul were excavated in 1962-69 and the restored ground plan can now be seen next to the existing cathedral. The installation of Bishop Wine in 662 or thereabouts, a man who, though ordained in Gaul, was a Saxon who spoke the king's language, marked the establishment of the second episcopal seat in Wessex.

Agilbert, according to the story, was highly offended at the division of the see and went back to Gaul, where he became bishop of

Paris. There is no record of West Saxon bishops at Dorchester from this time on and, for a period, there was no West Saxon bishop at all, for Wine was expelled from Winchester and went to London. Cenwalh sent his apologies to Agilbert, in Gaul, asking him to return, but the bishop declined, sending his nephew Leuthere, a priest, instead. He was consecrated bishop by Theodore, Archbishop of Canterbury, and became the fourth bishop of the West Saxons, based on Winchester.

For a period of a hundred years or so Dorchester and the surrounding region were under the control of the kingdom of Mercia and Mercian bishops were established at Dorchester to look after the territory to the north of the Thames, which had previously been West Saxon. Mercian control of the area was reaffirmed at the battle of Bensington (Benson) when the West Saxon king Cynewulf was defeated by King Offa of Mercia. Dorchester, now on the extreme southern frontier of the Kingdom of Mercia, was clearly inconvenient as an episcopal centre. Dorchester's Mercian bishopric came to an end and Mercian ecclesiastical administration was divided between the bishops of Lindsey and Leicester. These arrangements made sense so long as the political integrity of Mercia was maintained, but Danish raids in the 870s smashed the political and military power of the Kingdom and the episcopal administration also failed. The see of Lindsey came to an end and Leicester became unsafe. The Leicester bishopric was therefore transferred back to Dorchester.

Thus for the third time, Dorchester became a Cathedral centre, whose diocese extended throughout the Midlands, from the Thames in the south to the Humber in the north. This diocese, with its centre on its southern edge, was obviously a geographical absurdity but since it provided the bishop with some measure of security the arrangement made good sense. In fact this Mercian see survived for two hundred years or so, despite the resurgence of power under Alfred and his son

Edward the Elder, and at the time of the Norman Conquest Wulfwig was bishop. He was an old man and was allowed to retain the bishopric until his death in 1067. Remigius, a Norman, was appointed bishop but barely had time to get to know his new see before the bishop's seat was moved to Lincoln sometime between 1072 and 1086.

There has been considerable speculation as to the whereabouts of Birinus' church in Dorchester. Recent excavations at Wells (Somerset) have shown that the Anglo-Saxon cathedral there probably consisted of a 'cluster of churches' on a different alignment to the present Norman building (begun 1180) and this possibility must also be considered at Dorchester. The fact that the cloister garth of the later medieval abbey lay to the north, rather than to the south, of its church, may imply that there was some obstacle to the south, and this obstacle may have been the ruins either of Birinus's church or of the Mercian cathedral. There are, however, alternative explanations for the location of the cloister, which will be considered later. However, for North Elmham it has recently been convincingly argued that what was considered to be the 11th century cathedral is in fact a Bishop's chapel built after the transfer of the see to Thetford (c.1071). It therefore seems probably that the Saxon cathedral at North Elmham was a timber-built structure, possibly represented by the post-holes found during the excavation of the site. Again the possibility that the original cathedral at Dorchester was of timber construction cannot be ruled out, although the ready source of building material from the Roman town makes it more likely to have been of stone or even brick.

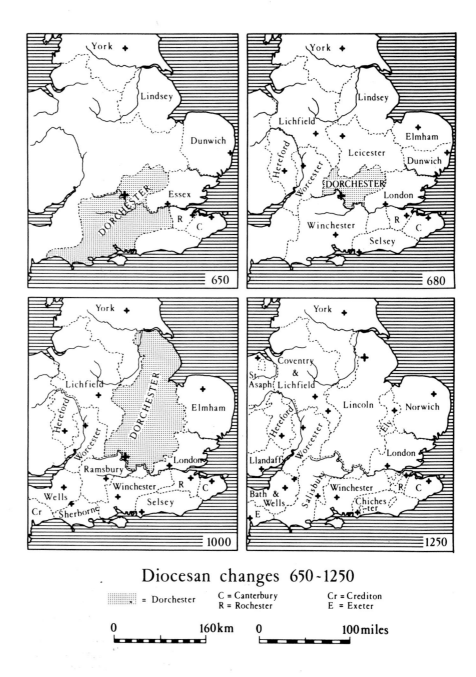

Diocesan changes 650~1250

▒ = Dorchester

C = Canterbury
R = Rochester

Cr = Crediton
E = Exeter

0          160km        0          100 miles

# Dorchester in Decline: the Late Saxon Period

**Tom Hassall**

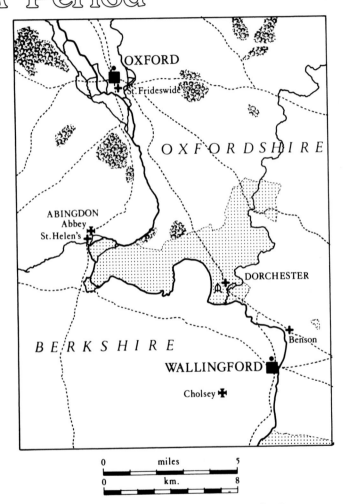

## The Dorchester Region in the 10th Century

- ■ Burhs
- ● Mints
- ⚐ Episcopal See
- ⬚ Land in Dorchester Hundred
- ✚ Benedictine Monasteries
- ✛ Minsters & other important churches

When the first bishopric had been established Dorchester's temporary political importance under the West Saxon Kings had dictated the choice. However the establishment of the third bishopric cannot be taken as a sign that Dorchester had any secular importance. The choice was dictated by pragmatism, combined perhaps with an element of antiquarianism. There is no evidence that Dorchester had retained its earlier regional role. The best measure of Dorchester's decline is that from this period onwards it was Oxford and Wallingford that emerged as the two main administrative and military centres of the region. The rise of these two towns, at the expense of Dorchester, can be seen by looking at the way in which the Danish domination of Mercia was replaced by the power of Wessex.

The re-emergence of Wessex was the work of Alfred the Great (871-899) and his son, Edward the Elder (899-925). One of the chief means by which West Saxon royal control was maintained in Wessex and established in Mercia was by the organisation of a system of regional fortified centres known as *burhs*. The *burhs* ranged in size from small forts to much larger fortresses capable of providing communal defence for a resident population as well as providing a place of refuge for the neighbourhood. Of the larger fortresses many, like Winchester or Exeter, took advantage of pre-existing Roman defences, while others had their defences laid out for the first time. The system of *burhs* reflected the military and political realities of the time and there was no room for antiquarianism or sentimentality.

Control of the Thames seems to have been vital to the strategy of Wessex since it formed the Kingdom's northern frontier while the major river-crossings provided access for an advance into Mercia. If Dorchester had retained any secular importance at all it would have been the obvious place for the establishment of a *burh*. It had after all no less than three ready-made fortified sites near the crossing of the Thames: the Iron Age hill fort at Wittenham Clumps, the Dyke Hills *oppidum* and the Roman defences themselves. None of these sites was chosen. The conclusion is therefore inescapable that the Roman north-south road was no longer of any strategic or commercial significance. Only Dorchester's episcopal tradition had prevented it from becoming abandoned like the Roman towns of Alchester to the north and Silchester to the south.

Instead of Dorchester becoming a *burh* Wallingford and Oxford were chosen and became the respective administrative centres of Berkshire, south of the Thames, and Oxfordshire, north of the Thames. In both cases it was probably their fords which were the decisive factor in their choice, although they may already have begun to assume some regional administrative role. The early history of Wallingford is obscure. There is evidence of extensive Roman occupation west of the town and antiquarians considered that its earth ramparts and rectangular plan were of Roman origin. However excavations have confirmed that the town's defences, best seen in the Kine Croft and the Bull Croft, are of West Saxon construction and, by implication, its street pattern is of similar date. However neither documents nor archaeological evidence can yet show whether Wallingford was either an entirely new foundation or else an existing settlement in the earlier 9th century.

The evidence for the rise of Oxford is rather clearer. There was no major Roman settlement at Oxford but by AD 730 a minster church had been established by St. Frideswide. This foundation probably attracted a lay settlement around it as happened at contemporary Abingdon. The archaeological evidence from Oxford also suggests that it was the regularising of the crossing of the flood plain of the Thames by means of embankments and fords over the various branches of the Thames which has led to the town's growth. The north-south road from the West Saxon port of Southampton which led into Mercia at Oxford

reflected the commercial and strategic realities of the time in a way which the old Roman road through Dorchester did not. Like Wallingford, Oxford was provided with an earth rampart and its grid of central streets lined with late Saxon buildings can also be shown to date to the early 10th century.

The commercial importance of the fords at Wallingford and Oxford, coupled with the towns' administrative functions as the chief towns of their respective shires, ensured their success, even after the victory of Wessex over the Danes and the end of a need for defence.

Dorchester's episcopal role and its tradition must still have given it a status which its brash neighbours can never have achieved. Apart from its spiritual role Dorchester would also have had an important role as the administrative centre of the bishop's estates. In the 10th century the lands of the see of Dorchester were grouped for administrative purposes into three areas which were in turn divided up for taxation purposes into a hundred smaller units known as hides. These hundreds were based in Dorchester itself, Banbury and Thame. The hundred hides of Dorchester consisted of the bishop's estates at Dorchester, Chislehampton, Clifton Hampden, Culham, Burcot, Drayton St. Leonard, Stadhampton and detached estates at South Stoke, near Wallingford, Fifield in Benson and Epwell near Banbury. It is likely that Dorchester, Banbury and Thame were grouped together in order to provide ships for naval defence. This is an arrangement which dated from King Edgar's reign (959-975), of whom it was said "he put his fleet on his enemies necks, and that surrounding peoples, especially island princes and tyrants (presumably Vikings) were terrified of him". Edgar is also reported to have perambulated the British Isles with a strong fleet each year at Easter. This fleet was probably one which was prepared each year to meet the Viking threat. Such a system might seem rather bizarre; however the Thames was at this time navigable from its mouth to Oxford so that Dorchester might not have seemed quite so remote from the sea.

However nothing could revive Dorchester's

fortunes. Oxford and Wallingford continued to expand in the 10th and 11th centuries and their success must have increasingly emphasised the anachronism of the bishopric, geographically on the edge of its diocese and set amongst the remains of the Roman town. The final move of the bishop's seat to Lincoln must have been inevitable and although the town's fortunes must have been given a considerable boost by the Bishop of Lincoln's foundation of the abbey, centred on the former cathedral, in about 1140, the effects of this on the prosperity of the community are largely unrecorded.

# The Abbey and its Buildings

James Bond, Nicholas Doggett, Julian Munby and John Rhodes

*Entry in Domesday Book, 1086, detailing the holdings at Dorchester of the Bishop of Lincoln.*

The Domesday Book shows that although Dorchester had lost much of its former importance by the end of the Saxon period (and lost more when the bishopric was removed) it continued to have a special significance as the chief of the Bishop of Lincoln's estates in this area. In 1086, the Bishop's own estate had almost doubled its pre-Conquest value, from £18 to £30, with additional assets — the mill rendered 20s, the fisherman paid 30 sticks of eels, and a half-hide of land produced another 12s; meadowland was worth 40s. There was also underwood six furlongs in length and three furlongs in breadth, the location of which is unknown and may not have been in Dorchester. There was a home farm with land for four ploughs; the remainder of the land was in the hands of the bishop's peasant tenants, with fifteen ploughs between them.

During the earlier part of the Middle Ages, the bishop regularly visited his Dorchester estate, expecting it to support him in residence there and at his other manors locally. The list of services required from the bishop's tenants, recorded in a thirteenth century survey of his estates, reflect the agricultural life of medieval Dorchester — ploughing, harvesting and carting the grain, stacking and tossing the hay, cutting and preparing wood for carting; two services were for making hurdles for the Bishop's sheep fold, and others for building byres and fetching wood for fencing from the Abbot of Eynsham's wood at Woodcote. Some produce was evidently sold off the manor — six tenants had to cart the grain from the field, carry it to Oxford and Wallingford for shipping to London and stay on the boat with it if necessary.

### The Eleventh Century Church — are parts of it still in existence?

Although the Victoria County History says that none of the existing Abbey church building contains work earlier than c.1180 it has nevertheless been suggested that there may be considerable portions of late-Saxon or immediately post-Conquest fabric in the present structure. One piece of evidence from the earlier church is that masonry in the north wall of the nave below the string course is different to that above it. The Reverend Thomas Barns, who was the first to make this observation, during the restoration in the 1870s, wrote of this and the masonry in the wall under the south-west window of the south choir aisle, that it is of the ' . . . peculiar wide jointed (sort) . . . characteristic of eleventh century work'. He also noted that the same kind of stonework appears on the east pier of the rude round arch on the south side'. Unfortunately the walls in question have now been re-pointed externally and are covered with plaster inside, but there appears no good reason to doubt Barns's statements, which were augmented by those of W.C. Macfarlane, that these walls do belong to an earlier church. Indeed, although the changes in masonry visible outside are not in their original state, they cannot have been entirely caused by re-pointing. Barns also claims that the absence of buttresses on the north wall of the nave — present in the twelfth century north choir wall, and now visible in the angle between that wall (the south wall of the thirteenth century north choir aisle) and the chancel — is proof of its eleventh century date.

This evidence led Barns to reconstruct the plan of the eleventh century church as follows:

An aisleless nave was of the same length as the present, with a choir in the crossing under a shingle lantern tower. A transeptal chapel stood on either side of the crossing and a shallow apsidal sanctuary to the east. This indeed would seem to be a reasonable proposition — it is unlikely that the squat crossing arches would have been strong enough to support a proper tower but would have been sufficient to allow the erection of a shingle lantern like those at Breamore (Hants),

Checkendon (Oxon) or, on a larger scale, at Edward the Confessor's Westminster Abbey. The high altar would have been under the crossing as in the late tenth century arrangement at the old Minster, Winchester.

Possibly the best evidence for the remains of an earlier church in the present building is in the form of the curious ledges, low down on the east faces of the round-headed lateral arches to the crossing. The arches themselves, although they might at a cursory glance appear to be Saxon, cut through the twelfth century string course referred to above, and are in fact seventeenth century in date. As Barns points out, the ledges are too low to form the 'abaci' of even the low arches below the level of the string course, which must have led to the transeptal chapels in the postulated eleventh century church. Although it is possible that the ledges are a result of the arches having been cut back at a later date, the plinths are very

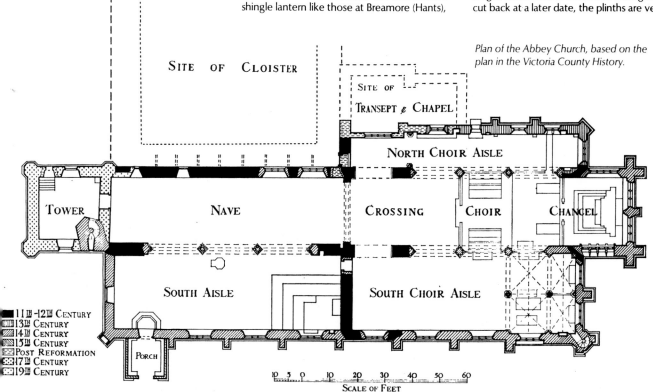

*Plan of the Abbey Church, based on the plan in the Victoria County History.*

SITE OF CLOISTER

SITE OF TRANSEPT & CHAPEL

NORTH CHOIR AISLE

TOWER

NAVE

CROSSING

CHOIR

CHANCEL

SOUTH AISLE

SOUTH CHOIR AISLE

PORCH

11ᵀᴴ-12ᵀᴴ CENTURY
13ᵀᴴ CENTURY
14ᵀᴴ CENTURY
15ᵀᴴ CENTURY
POST REFORMATION
17ᵀᴴ CENTURY
19ᵀᴴ CENTURY

10 5 0 10 20 30 40 50 60
SCALE OF FEET

*Effigy on the tomb of the unknown knight in the south choir aisle of Dorchester Abbey, about 1280; from Skelton's 'Antiquities of Oxfordshire'.*

regular and, as Barns suggests, may have served as altars flanking the entrance to the apsidal sanctuary. If this is the case we must accept that the lateral arches have been entirely re-built and were once much narrower to allow them to fit beneath the level of the later string course, which was presumably the eaves line of the eleventh century building. This must also be the case even if the ledges did not form altars and are merely the result of the arches being cut back.

Although there might appear to be little evidence for the existence of altars in this position, there are in fact quite good parallels for just such an arrangement at other churches of this period. At the eleventh century cathedral church of Sherborne the Royal Commission on Historical Monuments suggests that there may have been altars flanking the entrance to the choir on the 'deep eastern responds on the central crossing arches', an arrangement which is also found at St. Riguier in Picardy, the church on which the Commission based its Sherborne reconstruction. A similar grouping of altars is also known to have existed at the twelfth century churches of St. Martin, Wareham, Bere Regis and St. Benet, Cambridge. The liturgical aspects of ecclesiology are areas that have been neglected by archaeologists for too long.

If we accept that these features are part of an eleventh century church we must then ask who was the builder of this church. Barns favoured Remigius (the first and only Norman Bishop of Dorchester), who, according to William of Malmesbury, had plans for the re-building of the cathedral before the see was removed to Lincoln. It is not known if this work was ever started but Remigius' reputation as a builder is well known from Lincoln. It seems possible then that he did intend to re-build the church at Dorchester but when the work was left undone, it was completed as a parish church (as the church seems to have served until the foundation of the abbey in 1140). There is also an unsubstantiated statement by Anthony a Wood that Remigius built the first abbey (sic)

at Dorchester. Certainly too little is known of what happened at Dorchester between the decision to move the see in the 1070s and the consecration of the cathedral at Lincoln in 1092.

An alternative builder of the eleventh century church is one of the two Bishops named Fadnith who held the seat in the first half of the eleventh century (1004-16 and 1034-49). It is known that one of these two men re-built the minster church at Stow (Lincs) to serve the northern part of the diocese, and, as MacFarlane argued, it seems unlikely that, this being so, he would have ignored his episcopal church. It is perhaps not co-incidental that Stow is also cruciform in plan with transeptal chapel, although here the tower is of massive proportions.

Before leaving the eleventh century church one final speculation may be permitted. In 1657 Anthony a Wood wrote '. . . in digging at the west end of the church there was discovered a small vault that would hold three or four men or more, and at the top was a tonnell, like unto a chumney but something larger (which) when the abbey was standing . . . did go to the uppermost rooms'. What this building was it is difficult to say but did the late Saxon cathedral at Dorchester, like those at Sherborne and the Old Minster, Winchester, have a west work?

The church at Dorchester survived the removal of the Bishop's seat to Lincoln. Although most of the original endowments of the Dorchester diocese, including the rich Oxfordshire manors of Banbury, Cropredy, Thame and Great Milton, were transferred to the new Diocese of Lincoln, Remigius, the first Norman bishop, did allow Dorchester to retain some of its ancient liberties. Before the Conquest the income from a number of the chapels in the surrounding villages had been granted as prebends to the secular canons who served the cathedral. After the see was removed, Dorchester and its surrounding chapelries continued to be served by secular canons, and this area formed the nucleus of an ecclesiastical peculiar which remained exempt from the jurisdiction of the archdeacon.

Secular canons continued to live at Dorchester until about 1140. Bishop Alexander then decided to refound the church as a house of regular canons following Augustinian rule. The Augustinians had spread rapidly in England after the beginning of the twelfth century, and they were to acquire five other houses in Oxfordshire, the most important of which, Osney, was the richest monastic house in the county. Dorchester was settled by an independent branch of the order, canons of the order of St. Nicholas of Arrouaise, a house near Bapaume in Artois, whose austerity and strict observance of the rule was strongly influenced by contemporary Cistercian models. In England the Arrouaisian canons were largely confined to the Lincoln diocese; but they preferred remote rural sites, and soon after Dorchester had been settled some of the canons moved on to Shropshire, first to Tong, then to Lilleshall.

### The Abbey Buildings

As we have already seen little is known of the pre-Conquest church and the earliest buildings now standing on the site are those of the twelfth century canons' church. It is noticeable that the medieval cloister was on the north side of the church, a plan most unusual in Augustinian houses but shared by St. Osyth's Priory (Essex), itself originally a Saxon nunnery. Although it is possible that the gently sloping ground to the south meant that the conventual buildings could not be constructed on this side, it is more likely that this reflects the arrangements of the original buildings of the College of secular canons established alongside the cathedral. If the abbey had been built on a fresh site in the 12th century, the church would surely have been placed a little further to the north in order to allow the cloister to be laid out to the south, on the usual Norman pattern. Also it is perhaps not co-incidental that the conventual buildings of Sherborne Abbey (originally founded c.705) lie to the north, again for no obvious reason. Another

possibility is that ruins of one of the earlier cathedrals still stood in the way south of the abbey church.

The twelfth century church was of cruciform plan with a long, simple nave without aisles and lit by high round-headed windows, of which one and traces of more survive in the north wall. Perhaps from the first, as was the case in the later Middle Ages, the nave was used as the parish church, though there are said to have been other parish churches in Dorchester. At the crossing there may have been a tower, but only the west arch is now left. The transepts probably had eastern chapels, and have mostly been lost in later alterations, except for the plain west wall of the south transept, and a door to the cloister in the west wall of the north transept. The choir, where the canons' stalls were, and the east end have all vanished with later rebuilding, though there is external evidence that the Norman church extended as far east as the present choir aisles.

The cloister and all its associated buildings lay to the north of the church and their plan is unclear, though there will have been a standard monastic plan with chapter house, refectory, dormitory and so on, with other outbuildings beyond, like the barns that stood until recent times.

One rare survival of the Norman church is the lead font of c.1170, depicting the Apostles seated round an arcade.

During the early thirteenth century aisles were added to the choir, that on the north still surviving, with indications that it was first covered with a stone vault (though the aisle was altered later in the century and given new windows). The status of the church was enhanced by the opening of the tomb of St. Birinus in 1225, and the abbey was able to become a place of pilgrimage, raising money to start an extensive rebuilding programme around 1300 that led eventually to the building of a new shrine for the saint.

To this period belongs the remarkable stone effigy of an unknown knight of c.1280 in the south choir aisle, a recumbent figure in chain

*The lead font of the Abbey with a detail of its arcade, engraved by Orlando Jewitt for Henry Addington's Account of the Abbey Church, 1845.*

mail given a vivid feeling of movement by his crossed legs and hand about to draw his sword. Some of the stained glass in the church is also of thirteenth century date, including a figure of St. Birinus in the east window of the north choir aisle.

The great rebuilding of the church began c.1300 with the enlargement of the north choir aisle, already mentioned, with its new traceried windows and large three-bay arcade opening off the choir. Soon afterwards in c.1320 the south choir aisle was added, with a similar three-bay arcade, though differing in details. The aisle was wide, with 2 × 2 bays of vaulting at the east end, restored in the nineteenth century. This provided a spacious setting for the shrine of St. Birinus, built in 1320, destroyed at the reformation and reconstructed in 1964 incorporating parts of the original stonework. The new work was continued westwards, with the south aisle of the nave being added to the same width, doubtless as an enlargement of the parish church. Although the screen which closed off the nave from the choir was gone, the west wall of the south transept was left blank as a continuation of this screen, and was painted with a scene of the crucifixion, restored in the 19th century. A small door here allowed access to the shrine of the saint, beside the altar which is raised on the vault of a small charnel house built to hold the bones of burials disturbed in the building operations. The windows all along the south side of the church form one series, with intersecting cusped tracery, though the detailing of the buttresses on the outside is different in the choir and nave aisles.

The final phase of the rebuilding was the eastward extension of the choir by one bay in c.1340, the three new windows using a highly elaborate combination of tracery, sculpture and stained glass. The east window, unusually divided by a buttress and completely filled with cusped tracery, has a row of carved figures showing scenes from the life of Christ. The glass in this window now contains a

*The Jesse Window in the north wall of the Abbey chancel, illustrated by Skelton in 1823.*

variety of figures of saints and biblical scenes, some nineteenth century; it once contained the heraldic glass now placed in the south window, with arms of local noble families who were presumably benefactors of the church. The roundel at the top of the window is a nineteenth century restoration. The north window, known as the Jesse Window, has tracery in the form of a tree rising from the figure of Jesse at the base, with carved figures representing the ancestry of Christ. This theme was repeated in the glass, which is now only fragmentary. The south window has sculptured figures showing the funeral or translation of St. Birinus, and the glass that was here probably contained scenes from the saint's life, though this is not now in position. The richly decorated sedilia, or stone seats, below the window also have carved figures of saints and curiously shaped windows with stained glass in them.

The east end is a most important survival, with the design of stonework and glass united to form a single pictorial scheme. The brilliant inventiveness of the tracery and sculpture is unique, and quite outstanding in a national context. Together, the windows of the thirteenth-fourteenth century building programme at Dorchester form a history of the development of the Decorated style, from its geometrical origins, as in the north choir aisles, with parallels from as far away as Barcelona, through the cusped and intersecting work of the south front, parallelled at Merton College, Oxford, to the unique use of flowing tracery and sculpture in the east end of the choir.

Monuments of the fourteenth century include stone effigies of a judge, a bishop and a knight, all in the vicinity of the shrine, and there are several incised slabs and matrices of brasses of various dates. The few existing brasses include part of that of Sir John Drayton (died 1417) and an abbot with a possibly later inscription to Sir Richard Beauforest. Two of the bells are also of late-fourteenth century date.

The only later additions to the church were the west tower in the fourteenth century (rebuilt in 1602) and the late-medieval south porch.

## The Abbey Estates

All monastic houses depended upon endowments and grants of various kinds for their support and continuance. Their income was divided for taxation purposes into *Spiritualities* and *Temporalities*. Spiritualities included clerical income from tithes, glebe lands and mortuary fees. The Augustinian canons had particularly strong links with parish churches; Norman landowners often found churches a convenient form of gift, and because of this, the spiritualities contributed to the Augustinian economy to an extent which found no parallel in the affairs of other monastic orders. On the eve of the Dissolution

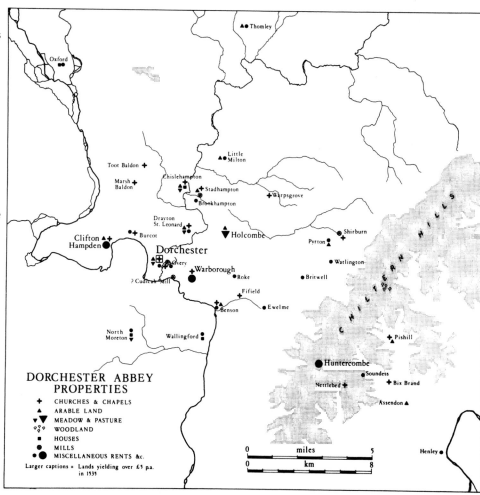

### DORCHESTER ABBEY PROPERTIES
✛   CHURCHES & CHAPELS
▲   ARABLE LAND
▼▼   MEADOW & PASTURE
°°°°   WOODLAND
●   HOUSES
●   MILLS
●●   MISCELLANEOUS RENTS &c.
Larger captions = Lands yielding over £5 p.a. in 1535

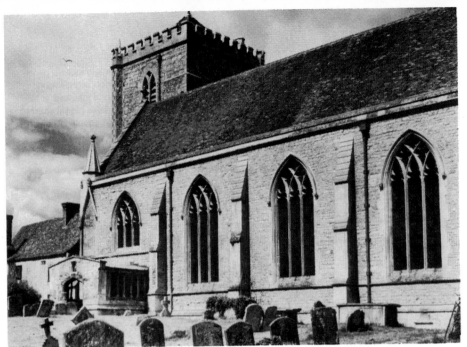

*The Abbey Church from the south.*

some 36 per cent of the entire wealth of the Augustinian order in Britain came from spiritualities. Temporalities, the income from landed properties, including demesne manors, rents, arable lands, mills, livestock and other farming resources, were correspondingly of reduced significance, though generally they still accounted for nearly two-thirds of the order's income. However, as the Augustinians had arrived in Britain only after the Conquest, they had missed the opportunities of acquiring wholesale grants of entire manors which had been the foundation of the wealth of the older Benedictine abbeys such as Abingdon; instead, their lands were usually made up by piecemeal gifts and purchases and by assarts and reclamation. Dorchester's income was even more biassed towards the spiritualities than the Augustinian norm; it had comparatively little landed property, and its income from spiritualities was always twice as much as that from temporalities.

There is no foundation charter for the Augustinian abbey of Dorchester, but there are two early papal confirmations of its possessions in 1146 and 1163 which indicate the nature of its original endowments. The papal bull of 1146 confirmed six chapels to the abbey. Five of these, Chislehampton, Clifton Hampden, Drayton St. Leonard, Stadhampton and Toot Baldon, had been part of the ancient endowment of the cathedral and had formerly been served by prebendaries (the ecclesiastical revenue of Dorchester itself also belonged to the abbey, but no vicarage was endowed and the abbey itself was responsible for ensuring that the church was served). To these chapels the Empress Maud had added the church of Benson with its tithes and appurtenances and a virgate of land (a virgate was a measure of arable land farmed by a villein tenant, averaging about 30 acres). The 1163 charter confirmed the abbey in its possession of these endowments and added the churches of Pishill, Shirburn and Marsh Baldon and the chapel of Fifield by Benson. The chapels of Overy and Burcot in Dorchester and the churches of Nettlebed and Warborough, which had originally been chapels of Benson, were probably included in these early grants, though not specifically named. Of the churches listed in 1163, control of Marsh

Baldon soon slipped from the abbey's grasp into the hands of the lord of that manor. Shirburn, though held by the abbey, never formed part of the Dorchester peculiar. The churches of Bix Brand and Warpsgrove, which had also apparently come into the abbey's possession by the end of the twelfth century, also remained in ordinary jurisdiction.

In some instances the abbey was able to increase its income from churches where it already held the advowson (the right of presenting priests to the benefice) by appropriating to itself all the church's revenue from tithes, glebeland and similar sources. Pishill and Shirburn churches had already been appropriated by Dorchester before 1220, and Bix was appropriated in 1275. Sometimes part of the profits of the living, often the small tithes (derived from hay, poultry and lambs rather than from the major commodities of corn and wood), were reserved for allocation to the vicar; and in 1301 the bishop gave licence for the churches of Bix, Pishill and Nettlebed to be served by chaplains instead of vicars, because of their poverty.

The taxation of Pope Nicholas IV in 1291 records that Dorchester Abbey's income from spiritualities was £58 18s. 4d, compared with only £26 1s 10d from temporalities (this compares with Osney's figures of £197 7s 8d and £224 9s 0d. respectively, £30 0s 0d and £75 5s 5d from St. Frideswide's in Oxford and £17 6s 8d and £49 0s 4d from Bicester Priory). The only other major record of ecclesiastical wealth is the Valor Ecclesiasticus of 1535, made very shortly before the Dissolution. Here Dorchester is recorded as receiving £124 17s 3d from spiritualities and only £65 5s 1d from temporalities, making a net total of just over £190 (compared with Osney's total of over £654).

Landed property, then, made up an unusually small proportion of Dorchester's income. However, the confirmations of its endowments in 1146 and 1193 do describe its estate in Dorchester itself in some detail. While the bishops of Lincoln retained control of the principal manor there, the lands which Remigius had reserved to the secular canons had been inherited by the Augustinian abbey.

*Interior of one of the great barns belonging to the medieval abbey, drawn by John Buckler in the early nineteenth century.*

The documents list land once held by Hunfredus the priest (later called Humfreys Mede) and a curtilage and croft which had belonged to the same priest; a place called 'Brademura' with its meadow and pasture; the bishop's court and buildings within the wall and the land beyond the wall extending to Dunning's house, including the bishop's granges and the croft beyond them; the bishop's garden and the furlong beyond it, extending from the ditch to Queenford Mill, comprising some 100 acres; the meadow bordering the river by the same land, and a meadow called *Suiftlac* on the other side; and the mill called *Cudicah* with the fishery and land belonging to it. Not all of these features can be located at present, but one might speculate whether the mention of an apparently substantial wall and ditch can be taken to imply that the Roman defences were still at least partly extant in the twelfth century.

Some of the 'granges' or barns and agricultural buildings north of the abbey survived into the seventeenth century, when Anthony a Wood described the 'great slatted barns, that are supported with buttresses', and part of the interior of one of these was drawn by John Buckler in the early nineteenth century. Two massive trusses are shown in his sketch, a base-cruck alongside the cart entrance and an aisled truss behind. A structure of this quality was very probably built by the abbey itself. Sadly, this magnificent building has now been demolished.

Outside Dorchester the abbey from an early date had a house with meadow and pasture at North Moreton in Berkshire; a hide of land at a place called *Cumba* which was probably the nucleus of its estate at Huntercombe near Nuffield; a house with a virgate of land and meadow and pasture in Chislehampton; a carucate of land at Pishill; 20 acres at Milton; the mill at Shirburn; and various other scattered lands.

During the course of the fourteenth century the abbey increased its landholdings. In 1279 the abbot had been undertenant of two virgates in Drayton St. Leonard and of four virgates at Holcombe near Newington. By 1346 the abbot had become the main tenant at Holcombe, and in 1535 held 173 acres there in demesne. This land had already been enclosed for sheep-farming following the desertion of the village of Holcombe, and 160 acres there were 'partly grown with thorns and fursens'. The manor or grange of Holcombe was then valued at £7 8s 8d a year. In 1329 the abbey acquired the entire manor of Huntercombe in mortmain. In Clifton Hampden the abbot had been an undertenant in 1279, but by 1346 had become one of the mesne tenants. By the sixteenth century

Clifton, too, had become one of the abbey's more valuable estates, yielding £7 2s 10d a year in rents. Smaller properties included Burcot, where the abbey had rights over four virgates in 1279 and increased its holdings during the fourteenth century by acquiring property, rents and farms, and Stadhampton, where, in the second quarter of the thirteenth century, the abbot was renting one of the two mills with one and a half virgates for 20s. The temporalities listed in the later 1530s included the whole manor of Holcombe, lands, tenements or rents amounting to properties in thirteen other places.

Finally the abbey had interests in some urban property. Canons of the Augustinian order were themselves instrumental in the development of a number of new towns and boroughs, notably at Dunstable and Kenilworth, and there are some indications that they may have attempted to promote similar commercial growth at Dorchester itself. The present course of the High Street includes the vestiges of a large triangular open space, now partly infilled, to the north-west of the abbey, which suggests an abortive attempt to lay out a new market-place in the Middle Ages. Alternatively this venture may have been the responsibility of the Bishops of Lincoln, who held the principal manor of Dorchester. The Oxfordshire towns of Banbury and Thame were both promotions of the Bishop of Lincoln. It is even possible that the Abbot and Bishop acted in concert, a suggestion which receives some support from the shape of the postulated market-place, which seems to lie in two distinct sections — a parallel situation existed at Pershore (Worcs.), where the abbots of Pershore and Westminster had market rights in common. No market charter for Dorchester is known, however, and whatever other attempts there may have been to promote Dorchester as a town appear to be undocumented. The abbey also had one house in Wallingford in 1163, and had interests in at least three properties in Oxford, the most important of which was Brid Hall, which stood on part of the New Bodleian site in Broad Street — this property was described as decayed and vacant in 1535.

48

## Abbey Life

Very little is recorded of the abbey's history, and what survives mostly comes from external sources, often emphasising the shortcomings of the monastic ideal. No doubt the canons looked after the spiritual needs of their parishioners in Dorchester and its dependent churches, either themselves or through vicars, and managed their small estates as well as they needed. But we learn of complaints, often made by disaffected individuals at Bishop's visitations, such as those in 1441 that the canons were hunting and fishing after dinner, or played chess and drank in neighbouring taverns. The abbot himself kept at least 5 mistresses at the common expence. Shortly after this it was reported that meals were rarely eaten in the refectory, but usually in the abbot's chamber, with lay folk of both sexes, and that half the canons were permanently absent looking after their churches. In 1445 it was said that Ralph Carnelle, one of the canons, regularly drank with the younger canons in the village, carried weapons like a desperado, and had given the prior a clout on the ear which left him permanently deaf. In 1530 it was said that the canons were late risers, often missing matins, that one canon, Thomas Witney, had attended church only three times during the year, spending weeks at his brother's house, or fishing and hunting, and that several times he had offered to fight the prior, that the grammar teacher was a drunkard, the buildings out of repair, the cloisters always open as a public thoroughfare and the parish church left open to the monastic church. Fragmentary as it is, the picture is one of a community open to human failings, and lax in the more severe aspects of regular life, but hardly a hotbed of flagrant immorality.

## Dorchester's Parish Churches

In 1542 Dorchester was visited by the antiquary John Leland who wrote that:
"of old tyme it was much larger in building then it is now toward the south and the *Tamise* side. There was a paroche chirch a litle by south from the abbay chirch. And another paroch chirch more south above it.

There was the 3 paroch chirch by south weste".
There is no earlier reference to these churches except William of Malmesbury's remarks on their magnificence, but it must be remembered that all the abbey records were destroyed by fire in the sixteenth century.

Gough, in the early nineteenth century, remarked that the foundations of one of these churches could be seen 'as you turn up to the bridge in the garden of the clerk's house'. A few years later Brewer wrote that he could see no such foundations but observed what he considered to be those of another in Farm Field. Neither of these sites can now be identified but the medieval skeletons recorded by R.A. Chambers to the north of the Old Castle Inn may be from one of them.

There is no real reason to doubt the existence of these churches, but Leland's statements on the status of churches may not always be completely trustworthy, as has been

*Inlaid floor tile from Dorchester Abbey, made at Penn in Buckinghamshire in the fourteenth century (British Museum).*

revealed from a study of the medieval parish churches of Wallingford. At Wallingford Leland says there were 14 parish churches — in fact there were 15 of which only 11 were parochial — which helps strengthen the suspicion that his 'paroch churches at Dorchester', while real enough, may not perhaps actually have been parochial.

Indeed, it is known that before the Dissolution, the parishioners of Dorchester worshipped in the south nave aisle of the abbey church, making, one would suspect, the use of other churches unnecessary. Were these churches then, already vanished by Leland's day, parish churches before the removal of the see to Lincoln (when the former cathedral church was first used for parochial worship) and did they become redundant after this date? Were they private chapels built in the Saxon period, or could they possibly be some of the many churches said to have been built by Birinus himself? Whatever their origins, only through the positive identification and excavation of their sites, will it be possible to ascertain their function and relationship to the Saxon cathedral.

The survival of the Abbey church is due to Sir Richard Beauforest, who bought the chancel at the suppression of the abbey in 1536 and gave it to the parish. Happily, as the surviving sculptures and glass show, damage through puritan zeal was not excessive, though the shrine of St. Birinus was destroyed. The monastic buildings mostly disappeared, though some fragments to the west of the church were incorporated into the Grammar School. The church was no more neglected than most parish churches in the following centuries, and was a considerable burden to the parish. The new tower of 1602 has already been mentioned, and later in the seventeenth century the roof of the south nave aisle was rebuilt and the north transept partly demolished. Major repairs were carried out in the mid-eighteenth century, and it was probably then that the vaulting over the site of the shrine was removed and plaster ceilings inserted in the place of the medieval roofs.

The revived interest in the study of gothic architecture in the nineteenth century led the Oxford Architectural Society to start a fund-raising campaign in 1844. Butterfield restored the chancel between 1846 and 1852, and Scott restored the roofs and vaulting between 1858 and 1874. Thus, in part, the present glory of Dorchester owes much to the nineteenth century, and many details of stonework or the location of glass can prove to be modern when closely examined or compared with drawings made prior to restoration. Fortunately, the gothic restorers worked from a better understanding of medieval buildings than many of their successors, and even if one subtracts their additions there is still an astonishing wealth of superb medieval craftsmanship to be seen in the church.

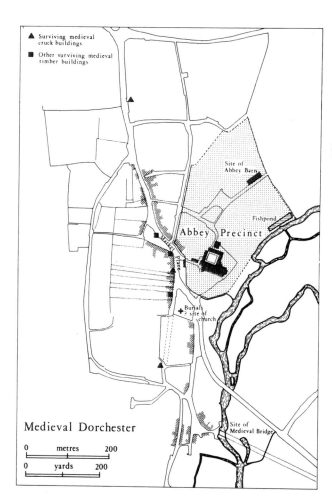

Medieval Dorchester

The medieval seal of Dorchester Abbey.

# Dorchester after the Dissolution

## James Bond and John Rhodes

Of the open-field system of medieval Dorchester, a considerable portion survived through to the Enclosure of 1861, especially in the north of the parish, and in Overy. The Tithe Awards and maps of the 1840s show the northern half still divided into parcels of strips, with the Great Common running downwards between them; there was still extensive meadowland along the banks of the Thame and Thames. By then however most of the land around the village had been divided and enclosed. Already by the sixteenth century it appears that some of the bishop's land was consolidated and possibly also enclosed; a lease of Bishop's Court in 1545 described land in blocks of 50 acres and 30 acres, with others of 20 and 10 acres. The lessee was Richard Beauforest, a substantial local farmer, who like many of his contemporaries was able to take advantage of the favourable conditions of the sixteenth century; in the subsidy of 1523, with 47 contributors, he paid over a third. Another of the bishop's tenants, Robert Hatchman, became the Crown's bailiff for the abbey lands at the dissolution, and also leased the bishop's land for a time. In the 1577 subsidy (which describes both of Beauforest's sons as gentlemen) amongst the most prosperous families were the Cherrills, yeomen of Overy, who remained as leading farmers in the village for three hundred years more.

The activities of these newly powerful local families were not always popular. In 1554 a yeoman and several labourers of Dorchester

## DORCHESTER & OVERY FIELD SYSTEM, c.1840

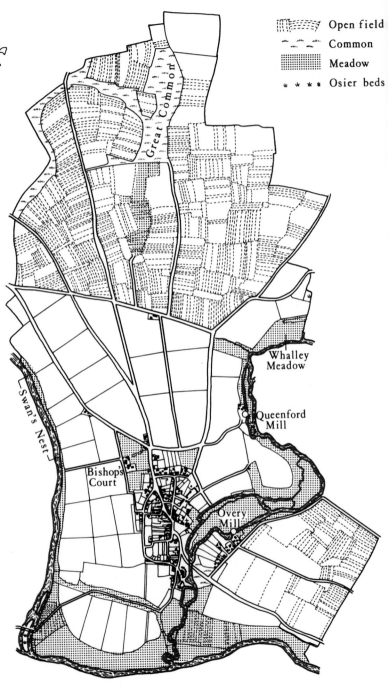

disputed Richard Beauforest's right to hold his lands in severalty, tore down the gates of Whalley Meadow and other enclosures, drove off his cattle and substituted their own. Other pasture and meadow land had by this time been enclosed by the abbey at Great Moynes, Little Moynes and Connyger, by the bishop at New Close, Mill Close and 'Swannesneste' Close ('Swan's Nest' survived as a field-name into the mid-19th century: Swan's Nest Piece lay immediately above the riverside meadows north-west of Bishop's Court).

Although it does not seem that there was any great movement towards converting arable into pasture (and the 1545 lease to Richard Beauforest actually forbade it) some conversion must have gone on to produce the large 40 and 50 acre pasture closes referred to in the seventeenth century. By this date there still remained three open fields, West Field, Middle Field and East Field, said in 1728 to 'Lye far from home' and all presumably in the north of the parish. A three-course system of two crops and a fallow was probably in operation in the 1600s, but experiments to make the open-field system more efficient were already under way, and by 1728 the fields were divided into four — three crops and a fallow. The system was criticised as making the land dry and requiring constant 'mucking and manuring'; Overy only had one field, which was cropped every year throughout the eighteenth century. In addition to the pasture and meadow closes and the open arable fields there were the commons, referred to in the sixteenth century as the Moor, the Cow Lease and Bridge Common with other common land along the road sides. The use of the commons required constant regulation; in 1634 presentments were made for keeping hogs in the cornfield and sheep in the Cow Lease.

By 1700 Dorchester was a larger than average village, and may have had a market of its own. It was not remarkable for its prosperity however, and in 1728 was described as "a poor town without any manner of trade nor likely much to improve". There were 79 householders returned for the 1662 hearth tax, but few were of any great consequence. Both the chief local estates were entirely let to tenants at this period, and the pattern in Dorchester almost right through the eighteenth century was of small to medium-sized farms. But by 1808, when Arthur Young listed 50 rateable farms, the pattern was changing; four substantial farmers already owned much of the land they occupied and were able to consolidate their position by the purchase of much of the Fettiplace estate, when it was sold that year. Part of their success lay in their willingness to experiment with new techniques. The Davey family in particular, farming most of Overy, were foremost in the movement, and helped to give Dorchester a reputation for good agricultural practice. William Davey was a founder of the Oxford Agricultural Society and was praised by Arthur Young "as one of the most intelligent farmers" in Oxfordshire. His son, George, carried on the tradition of successful and intelligent farming. In the 1840s and 1850s there were four major farmers in Dorchester — George Davey, with 400 acres employing 30 labourers; Joseph Latham at Bishop's Court Farm with 412 acres and 38 labourers and James Shrubb at Queenford Mill Farm with 600 acres and 40 men and boys (though not all his land was in Dorchester)., There was also the Cherrill family's Manor Farm with over 300 acres. Beyond these there were only a handful of lesser farmers, with a hundred acres or less. By the end of the century, the number of farmers had declined, and there were changes of ownership, but the pattern of a few large farms continued through into recent times.

*Overy Mill, Dorchester, in the 1930s.*

## Village Life and Occupations in the Eighteenth and Nineteenth Centuries

Farming dominated the pattern of occupations in the village as it dominated the landscape. In 1851 there were 120 agricultural labourers recorded (men and women) from a total village population of 872. Many of them were living at Bridge End, where there was also a concentration of paupers, some of them probably also farmworkers unable to find employment on the surrounding farms. The farmers themselves were still an important element in the community, with seven or eight recorded in the censuses and in the Trade Directories of the middle of the century, including those already mentioned. Their numbers had declined by the end of the century, though in 1891 three farmers were still resident in the village. Other occupations were directly connected with the life of an agricultural village: there was one corn dealer in 1851 and two millers. Of the three mills recorded in the early Middle Ages, there were two still operating in the nineteenth century.

Queenford Mill was apparently still working into the 1870s, but when it was sold in 1897 it had for some time been used merely as a store. Overy Mill, which had once belonged to Dorchester Abbey and later to the Fettiplaces, continued to work into the early years of the present century: George Cherrill was employing one Thomas Wheatley as miller there in the mid-nineteenth century.

Of the crafts supporting agriculture, the blacksmith and wheelwright were well represented. There were two families of blacksmiths in the mid-nineteenth century, the Howses and the Cobbs, and two wheelwright families, the Whichellos and the Jordans, providing employment for about eight men.

The one slightly unusual element in the village is the survival of many old-established inns and public houses. The Bull Inn was first recorded in the early sixteenth century, and its premises are still extant, though now divided into cottages. The Plough, Saracen's Head, Talbot, Crown, George, Swan and White Hart are all recorded in 1691. At least ten different inns are documented in Quarter Sessions records during the eighteenth century, and the keepers of the George and White Hart were sufficiently important in 1792 to have their own pews in the church. Further names had appeared by 1821, including the Fountain, Fleur-de-Lys, Horse & Hounds and Castle. At least half a dozen inns and public houses appear regularly in directory entries throughout the nineteenth century; in 1891 there was one commercial hotel (The White Hart), two inns (the George and Crown), and three public houses (the Plough, Fleur-de-Lys and Old Castle), in addition to three beer retailers. A minority of innkeepers also advertised that they pursued some other occupation: in 1850 two were also butchers, one a blacksmith and one a wheelwright. The continuity of some families in the trade is also striking: the Whichellos held the licence of the Crown at least from 1844 to 1891, and the Howse family similarly ran the Fleur-de-Lys

*High Street, Dorchester, about 1900.*

from about 1850 to the end of the century.

The largest group of shopkeepers and traders were those concerned with the retailing of food and drink; at any one time there were normally several butchers, bakers, grocers and beer retailers in the village. Four or five people usually found occupation in the building trades, as bricklayers, stonemasons, thatchers, plumbers or glaziers. In mid-century there was one cooper and one basketmaker (three areas of osier beds appear in the 1846 Tithe Award). Clothing trades of various kinds — drapers, tailors, hatters and sempstresses — were also present. The only other significant group of craftsmen were the shoemakers and cordwainers, of which there were often five or six at the same time.

Gentry, clergy, the independent classes and their servants made up the balance of the village population; there were schoolteachers, sub-postmasters, surgeons, veterinary surgeons, tax collectors and (in 1850) a river surveyor. A watch-maker and photographer was living in Dorchester in 1891.

Through the nineteenth century censuses one can see not only the pattern of employment in the village, but the existence of unemployment and pauperism; the picture is extended and detailed by the records of the Poor Law, with the earliest records surviving from the 1680s. Poverty in the parish was not serious in the seventeenth or the first half of the eighteenth century, though there were regular payments to support widows, orphans, the aged and the sick and for the less common misfortures — 1s. for pulling a women out of a gravel pit and 30s. for helping to keep Stephen Green 'out of ye Gaol'. A parish workhouse is mentioned in 1743 and there was smallpox in 1741 and 1753, ('To John Gable, Richd. Goodall for carrying William Banister out when he had the Small Pox and Digging the Hole — £0 — 4s — 0d').

From the 1770s, however, unemployment and the support of the poor were becoming serious and expensive problems. In the 1780s and 1790s work was found for the able-bodied on the roads, in the gravel pits and clearing snow, and payments were made to people for working on the surrounding farms on a daily

Dorchester Abbey Guest House, serving as the Grammar School when illustrated by J. C. Buckler in the early 1820s. The building now houses the Dorchester Museum.

basis. Cheap bread was sold to the poor, and wages topped up to allow families to survive. In the 1820s assisted emigration became a popular way of dealing with the problem, but in 1834 there were still 21 able-bodied men and 16 women being given regular payments, as well as 52 needy children and 39 infirm or totally disabled people to be supported.

Of the institutions of nineteenth century Dorchester, the most important were the church, the chapels and the schools. A grammar school was founded by Sir John Fettiplace in 1652, with an endowment of £20 a year for the schoolmaster, and the remains of the Abbey Guesthouse as schoolhouse. The statutes of the school survive and provide some interesting insights into seventeenth century education:

"The Schoole Master . . . shall be Master of Arts or att the least Batcheller of Arts of the University of Oxon .. . and able to instruct his Schollers both in Latine and Greeke in prose and verse and knowne to be sound in religion and of honest and Sober Conversation and if conveniently may be above Twenty three and under Sixty years of age"

" . . . and in punishing (he) shall neither beate his Schollers on the head nor pull them by the Eares Nose Cheek or Haire, Nor otherwise Knocke or Strike them intemperatley, but only beate them with a Rod . . . according to the quality of theire fault"

"That the Schoole Master shall not teach such as savour of Athisme, Epicurisme Popish Superstition or like Poysons".

Among the early scholars were sons of the Fettiplace and Lenthall families but by the mid-eighteenth century the school was in decline. In 1746 one Jacob Applegarth was appointed at only half the normal salary "by reaon of his not being sufficiently qualified to teach grammar", and the salary was continued at the low level. By the end of the century the school had long since ceased to function, but in 1801 a Mr. Paget advertised to re-establish 'Dorchester School' and by 1833 had 50 pupils.

In 1858 it was converted into a boys National School; a girls and infants National School had been founded in 1836, and the two continued independently until amalgamation in 1928.

In religion, there was a considerable choice in nineteenth century Dorchester. Roman Catholicism survived strongly in the village, due to a number of important yeoman families, principally the Daveys of Overy, and as the family prospered they were able to provide the community with considerable financial assistance. John Davey built the small church of St. Birinus at Bridge End in 1849. Protestant Nonconformity had a long history in Dorchester; a Baptist Chapel was built in 1837, and a primitive Methodist Chapel in Bridge End in 1839. Both had apparently closed by 1882, though remains of their buildings survive incorporated into private homes. Dorchester also housed a theological college, SS Peter and Paul's College for Missionary Students, founded in 1878 through the efforts of the Reverend W.C. Macfarlane, the wealthy and energetic minister at Dorchester from 1856 to 1885. The college closed in 1942.

Generally speaking nineteenth century commentators were disparaging about Dorchester. J.N. Brewer's *Topographical and Historical Description of the County of Oxford* (published in 1819) describes it as 'now humble in buildings and depending chiefly for its precarious resources on the traffic of the high road on which it is situated'. Pigot's Directory of 1842-4 states that 'The trade of the place is quite unimportant; manufactures there are none, and the market has for a long period been lost'. The Census Enumerator, in his preamble to the 1851 census, remarked that 'Dorchester was formerly a City of considerable importance, but is now strictly an agricultural village'. It had long since lost its status as a town and as a centre of commerce, and had not developed any distinctive trades or manufactures beyond the regular occupations likely to be found in any large village. Its position on two important communications routes, the Thames and the London-Oxford road, did, however, link Dorchester with a wider world and provided some variety in its social and economic life.

54

# Dorchester and the Outside World

**James Bond**

## Bridges, Fords and Ferries

There are no 'ford' place-names between Appleford and Shillingford, and no records of any medieval bridge over the Thames: whatever form the Roman road crossing over the Thames took, it appears to have become impassable long before the Middle Ages. The sixteenth century antiquary John Leland says that 'There was a ferrey at highe watars over Thames', which may imply that the river could still, however, be forded at low water. Elsewhere in his account, Leland refers to another ferry downstream from Dorchester, which may have perpetuated the site of the Roman road crossing, or may have been the precursor of the Keen Edge ferry about half a kilometre further downstream. There are occasional references to a ferry between Dorchester and Little Wittenham during the late seventeenth and early eighteenth centuries, and this was replaced by a wooden swing-bridge with a navigation opening about 6 metres wide, just below Day's Lock. The present 60-foot single-span iron footbridge was built in about 1870, at a cost of around £250.

The smaller River Thame was far less of an obstacle, and the earliest reference to a bridge over it occurs in 1146. In 1381 the Patent Rolls record a grant to the bailiffs of Dochester of pontage for a period of three years, to finance its repair. Further repairs were carried out in the mid-fifteenth century at the expense of Sir Richard Drayton and John Delabere, two local landowners. These repairs may have amounted to a near-complete rebuilding, for Leland recorded that 'The bridge of archid stone at Dorchester is but a new thinge to speke of'. He described it more fully as 'a very faire bridge of stone a little witoute the toune. The bridg is of a good lenghth: and a great stone causey is made to cum welle onto it. There be 5 principle arches in the bridge, and in the causey joining to the south ende of it'. Through the seventeenth and eighteenth century Quarter Sessions records there are numerous references to its poor condition and repair. An engraving by G. Hollis, published in the Gentleman's Magazine in 1818, shows the bridge at the end of its life, much as it was described by Leland, with five pointed arches of varying height with intervening cutwaters.

The medieval bridge was located some 100 metres downstream from the present crossing. The approach to it can still be traced as a short footpath to the east of the Bridge End green, with a slight causeway on the opposite bank, while foundations of its piers still exist below water level. It was finally demolished in 1816 after the completion of the existing stone bridge and causeway, designed by Francis Sandys, in 1813-15.

## River Thames: Navigation and Fisheries

The story of the Thames during the Middle Ages is dominated by the conflicts between three groups of people. The bargemasters who used the river as a great commercial highway required an unobstructed passage with a good depth of water: the owners and tenants of mills and fisheries were drawing off water and obstructing the course of the river with weirs; and the rest of the riparian population suffered flooding through interference to the river's course and destruction of fish through over-efficient barrages of kidells (Kidells were osier basket-work fish-traps, hence the expression 'kettle of fish'). From the eleventh century onwards there are records of attempts to enforce legislation to keep the navigation open by restriction and controlling the number and height of mill- and fish-weirs on the Thames. These seem to have been largely ineffective, and by the fourteenth century long stretches of the Thames above Henley were virtually unnavigable. In 1351 John Golafre and others were commissioned to survey all 'gorces, mills, stanks etc. between London and Radcot Bridge' to identify the main obstructions. In 1443 commissioners were appointed to locate kidells in the Thames between Burcot and Dorchester itself. Stow's *Survey of London* (1578-9) records 23 flash-locks, 16 mills, 16 floodgates and 7 weirs on the Thames between Oxford and Maidenhead.

The fishery of the Thames at Dorchester had belonged to the Bishops of Lincoln in the early Middle Ages, but in 1397 the Bishop granted all his fishing rights to Dorchester Abbey, along with those in the Thame. The eyots at Day's Lock and Little Wittenham Bridge may have been produced by medieval navigation cuts bypassing the bishop's and abbot's fish-weirs if they were not in existence at an earlier date. After the Dissolution of the Monasteries the fishery of the Thames was leased by the Crown to Sir Edmund Ashfield, from whom it descended to Edmund Fettiplace. Fettiplace is recorded as the owner of a weir and lock at Dorchester in 1580 and 1585, while at the same time a weir in Little Wittenham was owned by William Dunch. Dunch and Fettiplace were both members of the commission set up in 1605 to improve the navigation of the Thames, but the presence of weir-owners with vested interests on the commission limited its effectiveness. The Fettiplaces continued to have fishery interests in both rivers throughout the seventeenth century.: in 1691 their tenant held the ferry, fishery and lock at Dorchester for an annual rent of £4.

The section of the Thames from Burcot up to Oxford came under the control of a new commission in 1623, and this body was responsible for introducing the first pound-locks on the river. It was not until 1770, however, that the Thames Commissioners were reconstituted with powers of compulsory purchase and the legal right to acquire the old flash-locks and weirs and replace them with pound-locks. In August 1788 the construction of the first pound-lock at Dorchester was begun. It was completed by June of the following year at a cost of £1,078, and was named 'Day's Lock' after a prominent local Catholic family of yeoman farmers and fishermen. William Hallett, who had succeeded to the Dunch fishery interest at Little Wittenham, was ordered to remove his eel-bucks to make way for it (the bucks were the flood-gates in which the basketwork traps were set), and to keep the old flash-lock shut once the new lock was opened.

The improvements were not at first wholly successful. In 1791 Robert Mylne, surveyor to the Thames Commissioners, was expressing dissatisfaction with the conduct of James Batten, the lock-keeper, since he was paying more attention to the fishery than to the navigation. Mylne was also concerned about an obstruction in the river some distance downstream, 'At a place called Old Lock (which is the Remains of an old wear cross the River), many old Piles, whose heads are above the bed, and the Gravel which has accumulated round them'. The water was only two feet deep here, and Mylne wanted it dredged away. The exact site of this piling is unknown; while it may have been the ruins of an otherwise undocumented flash-lock, it is

*Constructing the new weir at Day's Lock, about 1885.*

G. Hollis dei et sculp.

*The new bridge built over the Thame in 1813-15, illustrated in 'The Gentleman's Magazine'.*

just possible that these were the surviving fragments of a timber bridge carrying the Roman road from Dorchester southwards over the Thames. Three years later Mylne was again complaining about the lack of water below Day's Lock, which had grounded three Thames & Severn Canal barges on their way upstream.

The first pound-locks built by the Commissioners had used cheap deal timber and sloping turf revetments, and soon began to deteriorate. By 1865 a surveyor was reporting that Day's Lock was 'in utter ruin: how it holds together I do not know. One of the gates is chained up; the weir is also out of repair, and in a very dangerous condition indeed'. In the following year the Thames Commissioners were superseded by the Thames Conservancy Board, which brought the whole of the navigable river from Cricklade to London for the first time under

unified management. The Conservancy began repairs to the ruined locks, rebuilding Day's Lock in its present form in 1871 and reconstructing the weir in 1885. Unusually, there was no lock-house at Day's Lock, and in 1882 a bell-push was installed, which for many years served to summon the lock-keeper.

Ironically, by the time that the navigation of the Thames had finally been set in good order, the need of the river for commercial transport had long since passed. While the extension of the railway network had taken trade away from the river, however, it had also made the river accessible to town-dwellers for recreation: and from the mid-nineteenth century onwards there was an enormous growth in pleasure boating. Public recreation has remained the main function of the middle Thames navigation to the present day.

## Roads

The Roman road system suffered almost total disruption after the fifth century, and although some lengths have survived as minor roads and farm tracks here and there, the modern road system is essentially based upon a network of new routes which came into existence during the Middle Ages. Three roads now entered Dorchester from the north, one from Abingdon, one from Oxford and a less important road from Drayton St. Leonard. To the south-east the London road, passing through Benson and Shillingford, entered Dorchester by the medieval stone bridge over the Thame. To the west, however, the Thames was a more formidable barrier, and could only normally be crossed by ferry. All the modern main roads (excepting, of course, the bypass) can be documented in medieval sources. The Bishop of Lincoln's tenants in the thirteenth century were required to cart corn to both Oxford and Wallingford. A survey of the Bishop's demesne in 1348 recorded ways to Burcot, Oxford, Baldon (the southern end of the old Roman road to Alchester may still have been in local use at this time) and an unidentified place called 'Wolden'. The medieval road towards Burcot and Abingdon was greatly increased in importance after the fifteenth century, for in 1416 licence was granted for the building of two new bridges over the Thames to replace the old fords at Burford and Culham which had been impassable and dangerous in times of flood; this had the effect of diverting much of the traffic between London and Wales away from the older bridge at Wallingford and up through Dorchester and Abingdon instead.

The increase of traffic, especially the more frequent use of wheeled vehicles, caused serious difficulties through the deterioration of road surfaces. The parish system of statute labour for road repair established under the Highways Act of 1555 was limited in its effectiveness, and by the eighteenth century a new system, based upon the principle that road users should pay for their upkeep, was coming into force. Turnpike Trusts, established by private Acts of Parliament and made up usually of committees of prominent local men, were empowered to set up tollgates to levy tolls upon travellers, the profits from which would then be put towards the maintenance of the lengths of road in their care. The road from Henley through Dorchester, Burcot and Culham to Abingdon was turnpiked under an Act of 1736; it was amongst the earliest turnpike roads in Oxfordshire, a fact which underlines its importance to through traffic. The heyday of the turnpike roads was in the middle and later part of the eighteenth century, but by about 1830 they were beginning to suffer declining income as much of their long-distance traffic was being diverted into other forms of transport. In 1874 the main road through Dorchester was finally disturnpiked. Two relics of the turnpike era remain, however. One of the trust's toll-houses still survives immediately by the south gate to the abbey churchyard: a small, single-storey red brick cottage on a stone base, hip-roofed with a central chimney-stack, with a half-octagonal projecting bay, the flanking windows of which give a view along the road in either direction. Its central doorway would have originally included a ticket-hatch. This building is aligned upon the road to the new bridge, and it must therefore have been added some eighty years after the road was first turnpiked. Marks upon its stone plinth show the height of floodwaters on November 1st 1828 and November 15th 1894. A few metres to the north-west is one of the milestones set up by the trust, givng the distances to London, Henley, Abingdon and Oxford; it is unusual in that its inscription has been recut: the mileage to London has clearly been altered from Roman to Arabic numbers (XXXXIX to 49), presumably to make it more readily comprehensible, and there are signs of other alterations lower down the stone, though these are now less legible.

The improvement of roads effected by the Turnpike commissioners gave a boost to the coaching trade. In the 1840s there were two coaches, the Defiance and the Rival, leaving the White Hart for Oxford in one direction and London in the other regularly twice a day. A carrier ran from the George to London twice a week and other carriers ran twice a week to Abingdon and one day a week to Oxford and to Windsor. The coaching traffic had ceased by the end of the century, but one carrier was still running a twice-weekly service to Abingdon and one day a week to Oxford and to Wallingford.

*Toll cottage south of the Abbey Church on the Oxford-Henley Turnpike.*

# Domestic Buildings in the Village

**Malcolm Airs**

By the second half of the seventeenth century, Dorchester was somewhat larger than the average village and evidently had a market. Some indication of its size is given by the hearth tax returns for 1662 which note seventy-nine householders. However, the recorded comments of contemporary observers continue to emphasise its unfulfilled urban potential. In 1728 it was described as a poor town without any manner of trade nor likely much to improve', and, as we have seen, James Brewer's county history, published in 1819, describes its buildings as humble and its economy as resting precariously upon the through traffic of the high road. Nevertheless, the architectural evidence for the period between these two unfavourable reports suggests that the town enjoyed a modest prosperity sufficient to encourage considerable building activity throughout the length of the High Street.

No doubt some of the money for these architectural improvements derived from the local agriculture, the efficiency of which was praised by Arthur Young in 1813, and which resulted in the total reconstruction of Overy by the Davey family during the course of the eighteenth century, but the presence of several important inns with stabling facilities in the High Street indicates a flourishing service trade which must have contributed handsomely to the local economy.

The road through the centre of the town had been of national significance since at least the Roman period and it continued to be important until Dorchester was finally by-passed in 1982. The dominance of the road is reflected in the present topography with an almost unbroken concentration of historic buildings along the length of High Street and Bridge End, and the other interesting buildings dispersed amongst twentieth century development in the minor streets and lanes to the east and west. The survival of so many historic buildings is a reflection of the lack of strong economic pressures for change in the mid-twentieth century and presents a particularly rewarding subject for closer study.

Since Dorchester lies on river gravels superimposed over Gault clay, there is no proper building stone anywhere in the neighbourhood and the variety of materials used to construct the town are a tribute to the ingenuity of the local craftsmen and to the potent influence of changing architectural fashions. The earliest surviving buildings in Dorchester are timber-framed and timber was almost the invariable building material down to the end of the seventeenth century. Today there are no significant areas of woodland within the parish. Timber is a heavy and difficult material to transport for any distance on a regular basis. Its use in the medieval period indicates its presence close at hand and presupposes properly managed woodlands in order to meet the building demands of the town. This is confirmed by two surveys of the mid-sixteenth century which show a total of around 2,000 trees suitable for building purposes on the two principal manors.

Most of the medieval buildings survive only in a fragmentary and much-altered state. However, a drawing of a barn in Dorchester made in the nineteenth century by J C Buckler gives an excellent picture of the quality of timber available in the early fourteenth century. Not only does it show massive scantlings for the timbers of the trusses and the plates, but even the vertical studs of the wall framing are substantial and square in section. The barn was of aisled construction with base-crucks instead of aisle posts in the bay defining the entrance. Such a hybrid form of construction was presumably devised to allow for greater manoeuverability in the area where the crops entered the barn and where the aisle posts might have hindered the movement of carts. Base-crucks, which are curved timbers extending vertically from near the ground to the underside of the tie-beam, are invariably associated with buildings of some social status and, although the precise location of the barn shown in the drawing is not given, it was almost certainly part of the farm buildings associated with the Abbey. At least nine of the twenty-three barns in England known to have had base-cruck trusses were built for monastic houses. The quality of the workmanship is quite exceptional for such a utilitarian building, with every principal timber

## MAP KEY

1 Cranmer Cottage
2 Tudor Cottage,
    76 High Street
3 Wall N of Willoughby House
4 Old Forge, High Street
5 9 Martins Lane
6 Willoughby House
7 63 High Street
8 The Crown Inn
9 The Bull Inn
10 55 High Street
11 36 High Street
12 Girls and Infants Schools
13 Abbey Cottage
14 Wall, Manor Farm Close
15 The White Hart
16 17 Watling Lane
17 Cob Cottage, Malthouse Lane
18 Malthouse Lane
19 37 and 39 High Street
20 Hallidays Antique Shop
21 33 High Street
22 31 High Street
23 2 Queen Street
24 The Vicarage
25 The Manor House
26 The George
27 The Priory
28 Lych Gate Cottage
29 13-19 High Street
30 Fleur De Lys Inn
31 Dorchester Galleries,
    Rotten Row
32 3 High Street
33 13 Rotten Row
34 Willow Tree Cottage,
    2 Rotten Row
35 11 Rotten Row
36 Terrace, Watling Lane
37 9 Rotten Row
38 8 Rotten Row
39 Terraces, Watling Lane
40 69 Watling Lane
41 Croft Cottage,
    2 Samian Way
42 Mollymops, Samian Way
43 Albert Terrace
44 71 Watling Lane
45 22 Bridge End
46 24 Bridge End Close
47 Bridge House, Bridge End
48 Bridge End Green
49 Thatched Cottage,
    Wittenham Lane

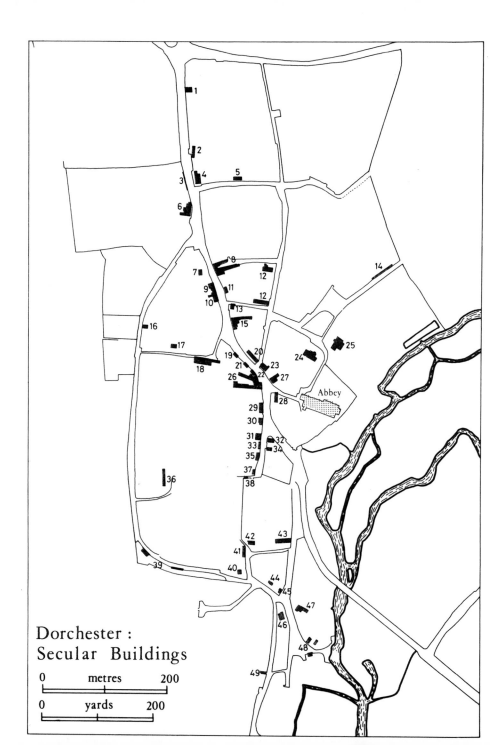

Dorchester :
Secular Buildings

0    metres    200

0    yards    200

carefully shaped and chamfered, and that in itself suggests a client able to afford the very best. In the circumstances of the time in Dorchester that client could only have been the Abbey. If this supposition is correct, the barn almost certainly survived into the seventeenth century when Anthony a Wood described some 'great slatted barns, that are supported with buttresses' to the north of the church, of which agricultural complex the neatly coursed length of stone walling forming the eastern boundary to the garden of the house called Tamesis in Manor Farm Close is the sad relic.

The drawing of the barn is the only evidence of base-cruck construction in Dorchester, but true cruck construction, where the curved blades rise beyond the tie-beam or collar to form part of the structure of the roof, is known from a number of examples. Tudor Cottage, 76 High Street, lies on its own just outside the built-up area of the

High Street and possibly it should be regarded more as a rural building than part of the town proper, but the terrace of cruck-framed cottages numbered 13-19 High Street is situated almost opposite the Abbey gate and is decidely urban in character. It is now sub-divided into four small cottages but in 1846 at the time of the Tithe Award it was in single occupation and described as 'House & Premises'. Despite the description, the street frontage was divided into three parts and that division is still apparent today with the steps up to the central portion marking the slightly raised level of the ground floor. A convincing reconstruction of the original arrangements awaits a full structural examination.

The other cruck-framed buildings in Dorchester present further problems of interpretation. Croft Cottage, 2 Samian Way, to the east of the High Street, was almost entirely rebuilt in 1981 but three mutilated

*13-19, High Street: a terrace of medieval cruck-framed cottages with later frontages.*

60

ades survive in the east wall of what is now a
ree bay structure. They are of substantial
antling with a smooth curve and they show
xtensive evidence of fire damage. However,
e purlin over the central bay showed traces
smoke blackening beneath the later
arring and it is possible that the building was
iginally a small hall house with an open
earth in the central bay. By 1846 it was
vided into two cottages with an attached
rn at the southern end, but it was almost
rtainly built as a single house, to which state
has now reverted. The High Street range of
e Fleur-de-lys contains the remains of four
uck trusses although the present waggon
trance in the southernmost bay is
esumably a later modification of the original
angement.

By analogy with cruck construction
sewhere in the region, all these buildings are
ely to be of medieval date. They have
rvived because they were substantially built
d because they were capable of adapting to
e changing fashions and domestic demands
subsequent ages. In adapting to these
anges, their original appearance has been
dically altered. Only close observation during
cent building works has revealed the
idence of their medieval structure. An
cellent example of this metamorphosis is
mber 13, Rotten Row, where a complete
nber-framed hall house with a rare internal
ty was discovered hidden behind a most
promising brick exterior when it was
odernised in July 1984.

Another range of disguised medieval
ildings is numbers 37 and 39 High Street.
ese are particularly important because the
rviving framework allows the reconstruction
the sort of small tenement that must have
ed much of the High Street before the
teenth century. They were originally built,
obably in the fifteenth century, as a single
ucture comprising three separate units.
ey are of box-framed construction with
h-braced tie-beams and alternating king
d queen strut roof trusses. Each unit was one
y wide with an entrance off-set to one side.
e internal arrangements are less easy to
cipher, but it seems probable that the

entrance led into a passage with a door off to a
front room operating as a shop or workshop
and a smaller room behind. There was
probably an upper chamber over the shop,
but the presence of smoke-blackening on the
wind-braces, which are all that survive of the
longitudinal members of the original roof,
suggests that part of the ground floor was
open to the rafters and contained an open
hearth. Two of the units were subsequently
amalgamated to form number 39 and the
original arrangements were swept away by the
insertion of chimneystacks and upper floors
throughout. Their appearance was further
altered in the eighteenth century when the
roof was raised to eliminate the old-fashioned
dormers and their timber framework was
covered with render as part of the general
High Street facelift. Number 37, however,
retains its ground-floor shop trading as the
Nook and provides an excellent indication of
its original proportions.

*37 and 39, High Street: disguised
medieval buildings of box-frame
construction.*

The Nook represents the smallest surviving medieval structure in Dorchester. The George Inn, by way of contrast, has always been one of the grandest buildings in the town. Situated in a prime position in the High Street, opposite the gate to the Abbey, the earliest parts were built at the very end of the fifteenth century or early in the sixteenth century. Like all the other medieval buildings in Dorchester it is timber-framed, with the original structure characterised by lower king strut roofs with through purlins, and deeply curved tension braces in the wall framing. The unity of construction makes it clear that the original parts of the existing building comprise the two double-gabled and jettied ranges fronting onto the High Street and the long wing extending to the west on the south side of the yard. The single gabled range with the

lower jetty at the north end of the street front was originally a separate dwelling house and is described as such in the 1846 Tithe award. The present bar was originally divided into two rooms on the ground floor, each with its own fireplace and there was a further heated room to the north beyond the archway (now the residents' lounge). All three rooms were probably separate drinking parlours and were no doubt differentiated by the fanciful names similar to inn signs which are sometimes found in contemporary inventories and which before the advent of a serving bar would have enabled the source of the orders to be correctly identified. Thus in the tavern scene in the Boar's Head in Cheapside in *Henry IV Pt 1*, Shakespeare has Prince Henry cry out "Anon, anon, Sir! Score a pint of bastard in the Half-Moon", and the serving boy calls out to

his colleague, when he is busy "look down in the Pomegranate, Ralph". The rooms above, all heated by their own fireplaces, were probably further parlours and private chambers.

The flat-headed archway is decorated with hollow chamfers and formerly contained security doors which could be shut at night. The south range in the yard beyond is a remarkable survival which is of great historic importance in that the original functions of its various rooms have remained substantially unchanged. The dining room at its western end where it joins onto the street range is the original medieval hall and it remains open to the underside of the roof as it has always done. Beyond, on the ground floor, is the kitchen in its traditional position at the low of the hall. The stabling which was originally placed beyond the kitchen has been replaced by more modern uses but the bedroom accommodation on the upper storey of the range remains in use. Access is provided by an outside staircase which leads onto an open gallery, giving independent entry to each individual room. The rooms were unheated and probably each originally contained a number of beds which would have been shared by several guests. Three bedrooms now survive but the open gallery originally continued to the west for the full length of the existing building where it no doubt served at least double that number of rooms.

The short range on the north side of the yard is later in date and the arch braces to its upper storey framing signal a change in carpentry techniques. The brick building beyond was converted from garaging into additional bedroom accommodation in 1981 and 1982 as part of a comprehensive and sensitive refurbishment carried out for the present owner. Amongst other discoveries the works revealed that the vanished west range which is shown on nineteenth century maps as closing the yard, and the truncated remnant of which is still attached to the galleried wing,

was a secondary feature of relatively flimsy workmanship. Dr Pantin's classification of the George as originally a courtyard inn, therefore, must remain open to doubt; no matter that it had become one before the middle of the nineteenth century.

The street elevation of the George was remodelled in the eighteenth century when it was given its present rendered appearance and interesting assortment of vertical and horizontal sliding sash windows. Almost certainly, it would have originally advertised its commercial presence by a lavish display of exposed timber-framing and ostentatious glazing, as did its rivals elsewhere in the street. The White Hart, for example, still shows something of its framework in the first floor of the tall, triple-gable block with its asymmetrically placed coaching entrance. Originally this had three projecting oriel windows tucked under the narrow second floor jetty, the evidence for which is provided by sawn-off tenons and glazing grooves in the vertical studs. In 1691 the wattle and daub infill between the windows was replaced by brick nogging laid in a decorative herring-bone pattern and in the eighteenth century the oriels were replaced by fashionable double-hung sash windows. The remainder of the inn was located in the lower brick building to the north and there was formerly a long range extending backwards at right angles as far as Queen Street and enclosing a narrow yard in similar fashion to the George and the Crown.

The Bull Inn on the opposite side of the High Street seems to have had a pattern of alternating deep and high windows set within the framework of its jettied upper storey in the range which contains its off-set coach entrance. The northern part of the building, now called Bull Cottage, is of a different date and the details of its original fenestration pattern remain hidden behind its eighteenth century render. Adjoining the Bull to the south is the best carpentered and most consciously designed timber-framed building in the High Street. It is three storeys high set above a low stone plinth. Both the first and the second storeys are jettied with carved scrolled brackets decorated with acanthus leaves,

*Left) The George Hotel: front elevation.*

*Below) Galleried range at the rear of the George Hotel.*

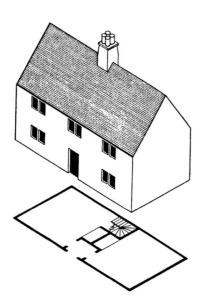

rosettes and miniature Ionic capitals in a deliberate classical fashion. A carved fascia board was formerly attached to the bottom rail of both jetties by secret tenons. The whole street elevation was designed with an eye to perfect symmetry that must have been quite startling when it was first erected. The massive chimneystack with four diamond shaped shafts arising from a rectangular base is placed in the centre of the roof and its position against the front of the house is marked by the blank framing of the central bay. To either side on both ground and first floors were projecting oriel windows framed into the undersides of the jetties and flanked by high windows in the plane of the wall. The flanking windows were restored and re-opened in 1983 but the oriels were destroyed when the front was inevitably rendered in the eighteenth century. No entrance doors were permitted to spoil the symmetry of the street elevation and the present entrance at the north end is a later insertion.

Internally, there were two large rooms on each floor separated by the central chimneystack. Access was by a generous staircase wing placed at right angles in the centre of the rear. The wing has subsequently been removed, but its former existence is confirmed by the evidence of blocked doorways at ground and first floor levels in the original rear wall. It seems likely that the ridge of the wing joined the main roof immediately to the rear of the chimneystack, which would account for the unusual location of the latter wholly within the front slope of the roof and the makeshift area of tiling behind the two rear shafts. Lacking any evidence for a principal entrance elsewhere in the building, it is possible that the house was entered through the vanished staircase wing. Such an arrangement would be unusual but cannot be discounted. Another possibility is that the whole building formed a self-contained addition to the Bull Inn, in which case an entrance from a common yard at the rear would be quite acceptable. The Bull was certainly in existence when the building was erected, for its flank wall forms the northern internal wall of number 55. But, on the other hand, there is no evidence that the buildings were ever in common ownership and by 1840 they were described as separate houses.

*(Above) Typical lobby entrance house with central stack.*

*(Right) The White Hart Hotel; the replacement of wattle and daub in the panels by decorative brick nogging is commemorated by the date — 1691.*

*5, High Street, built in 1610.*

According to an inscribed date underneath the position of the northern oriel window on the first floor, 55 High Street was built in 1610. Such a precise date is invaluable in demonstrating that good quality timber-framed buildings with ostentatious fenestration and prominent chimneystacks were being built for fashionable citizens in the early seventeenth century. It also indicates a level of prosperity that was able to afford both intricate carved decoration and lavish quantities of window glass.

At about the same time and perhaps slightly lower down the social scale, there is evidence of new house types appearing to meet the changing domestic requirements of the time and suggestive of accumulated capital being available for investment in building in the early seventeenth century. The open hearths of the High Street tenements such as numbers 37 and 39, had been superseded in buildings of a roughly comparable size by the third decade

of the sixteenth century if the date of 1527 inscribed above the fireplace in number 36 on the east side of the High Street can be accepted as referring to the installation of the chimneystack. However, it was only about a century later that the classic lobby entrance house with a central bay containing an entrance lobby, axial chimneystack and staircase, began to be built in Dorchester in significant numbers. All the medieval buildings considered so far, such as the inns and the High Street tenements, were uncompromisingly urban in form. Even 55 High Street with its tall, double-jettied, facade and its prominent fenestration pattern, is clearly a town building. The lobby entrance house, however, is essentially a rural building type which originally evolved as a detached structure surrounded by open land, and it is in this form that it first makes its appearance in Dorchester. The Old Forge to the north of Martin's Lane on the east side of the High

Street still looks like the farmhouse that it once was. It is a large timber-framed house which has been further extended by a slightly lower rubble-stone wing to the north. The original building is strongly symmetrical around its central entrance and is crowned by a proud display of chimneys rising from the middle of the roof. The chimneystacks are ranged in a row of three diamond-shaped shafts at right angles to the axis of the roof. Both ground floor rooms are heated, but only one of the first floor chambers had its own fireplace. The dormered attic rooms were unheated. This selective heating arrangement is characteristic of other lobby entrance houses in Dorchester and, although it clearly marks the relative importance of the various rooms, it remains somewhat puzzling as the provision of an additional chimneyshaft was neither technically difficult nor financially onerous.

Once the advantages of a draught-free entrance, independent access to the ground

33, High Street.

Abbey Cottage.

floor rooms, the possibility of fireplaces in all the important rooms, and a convenient position for the staircase were established, lobby entrance houses proliferated in the town. Those of the seventeenth century invariably were timber-framed, such as number 9 Martin's Lane and number 33 High Street. The latter is of a similar size to the Old Forge, although it lacks an attic storey. Situated within an unbroken street frontage at the heart of the town, it is far more urban in feel than any of the other houses of a similar type in Dorchester and this impression is reinforced by the wagon entrance on the north side which links it to the adjacent cottage. Abbey

*The Old Forge.*

Cottage, on the opposite side of the High Street is considerably smaller in scale and is marked out by its recently restored brick-nogging set in a herring bone pattern and its gable-end jetty overhanging the footpath to the north. Jetties are exceedingly rare on lobby entrance houses and this, together with the flimsy projection over number 31 High Street, must represent the final manifestation of a once fashionable tradition.

The suitability of the lobby entrance plan for those members of the community who could afford to build only on a small scale is demonstrated by the timber-framed and thatched example of 63 High Street which is set back from the road behind a cottage garden. The differences in the framework on either side of the doorway suggest that this building might have evolved into the fully-developed lobby entrance form in two stages. Certainly, other buildings in the High Street with different original arrangements, such as number 39, were adapted in the seventeenth century to provide the characteristic elements of the plan. Away from the main thoroughfare in Samian Way, Mollymops is dated 1701 and has a slightly offset chimneystack which only directly heated the major rooms in the house. It is

attractively built in alternating bands of brick, chalk and flint, and conveniently marks the rejection of timber as the major building material in Dorchester as the new century began. Within a very few years, the appearance of the town was totally transformed.

The timber frames of the existing building once fashionable but now clearly despised, were rendered over to give the appearance of stone and it is only in recent years that some of them, such as number 55 High Street, the Bull, and Abbey Cottage have been re-instated to something approaching their original form. The veneer of render on most them is so thin that it could never have been intended as anything more than an economic way of covering up what contemporary taste considered to be a vulgar show. The substitution of sash windows for the tradition leaded casements completed the disguise. Such superficial modernisation can be contrasted with the more full-blooded remodelling that took place later in the century and early in the nineteenth century when the Manor House was given a castellated parapet, Gothick windows and a matching porch, and Willoughby House received its deeply rusticated elevation and porch with Egyptian columns.

*lloughby House.*

chequer pattern of alternating vitrified headers and orange stretchers laid in Flemish bond can still be seen. The first floor, above a projecting band course, is almost entirely of vitrified headers, with only the window dressings and quoins in contrasting orange bricks. The odd asymmetrically placed pedimented entrance projection appears to be a later alteration rather than an original feature. Certainly the other large eighteenth century houses in the town sought a precise symmetry on their principal elevations and this was usually combined with a similar delight in the patterns that could be created with vitrified bricks. Dorchester Galleries, in Rotten Row, for example, has a fluted classical central doorway and a chequer-patterned brick facade, while the main elevation of Bridge House in Bridge End, is completely vitrified, with a delicate projecting Tuscan porch. 24 Bridge End Close, on the other side of the road, is dated 1797, and again demonstrates the cachet attaching to vitrified bricks, by utilising them for the whole facade. The mansard roof of this house, which enabled more generous accommodation at attic level is unique in Dorchester.

*24, Bridge End Close.*

The desire for a more acceptable building  terial than timber tempted some, such as  builder of Lych Gate Cottage, to  periment with the soft and inadequate  lk available in the neighbourhood, but the  ults were never really satisfactory and it is  erally found only in small quantities often  insignificant elevations. For most residents  eighteenth century Dorchester the  ionable new material was brick, and its  ictive oranges and reds enlivened with  ker vitrified headers provided an elegant  trast with the newly-rendered facades in  High Street. In some cases brick was used  n alternative method of disguising an  lier timber-frame, as can be seen at The  ry and the former Crown Inn, but more  mmonly it offered the opportunity for those  h sufficient funds to break completely with  past by demolishing their existing buildings  starting afresh in a more sophisticated  e. In the centre of the town this led to the  struction of some large and impressive  ses of conscious architectural pretension,  h as the premises now occupied by  idays Antiques, where the subtle  orative qualities of the contrasting colours  he local bricks were fully exploited. The  nd storey has been punctuated by  dern bow windows and shop signs, but the

*Decorative brickwork at Halliday's Antiques.*

*Cob and thatched wall, on the road to Oxford north of Willoughby House.*

*9, Rotten Row.*

*Typical house with central entrance and gable ends stacks.*

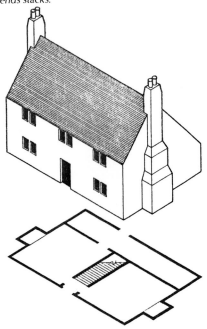

The eighteenth century boom in building was not confined to those able to commission such fine and elegant houses. It extended down through the social scale to the occupants of quite humble cottages. Even at these levels, symmetry was an important consideration although occasionally convenience dictated that it was not always exact. The lobby entrance plan offered a traditionally symmetrical form and examples continued to be built in the eighteenth century. Some like Cranmer Cottage in an isolated position at the north end of the High Street, were fashionably constructed of brick, others such as 11 Rotten Row could only afford brick for the publicly-seen elevations and had to make do with timber for the rest of the house. The great disadvantage of the lobby entrance plan when it was adopted for the smaller house was that the mass of the chimneystack took up a lot of space in the centre of the building which greatly restricted the size of the rooms and made the entrance lobby inconveniently small. Setting the entrance slightly to one side and reducing the number of flues so that the stack itself was smaller, as was done at 9 Rotten Row, only partly alleviated the problem. The solution, which became increasingly popular during the course of the eighteenth century, was to dispense with the central chimneystack althogether and to substitute two separate chimneystacks placed against the gable-end walls. If the central position of the entrance was retained this enabled an appearance of symmetry to be preserved whilst liberating the whole shell of the building for full domestic use. The staircase still tended to be placed in line with the entrance but was now of more

generous proportions particularly if it was housed in a projecting turret at the rear of th building. This arrangement can be seen best Willow Tree Cottage, 2 Rotten Row, which i built in chalk. Other examples are of brick an include houses of the nineteenth century su as 17 Watling Lane and 3 High Street, both o which have roofs of Welsh slate.

The eighteenth century Thatched Cottag in Wittenham Lane is one of the smallest houses in Dorchester with the gable end chimneystack plan and it represents a furthe step down the social scale. It is probably one of the earliest surviving true cottages and it i constructed out of the most basic available materials; cob and thatch. Cob is a moist mixture of earth and straw which is raised in layers to form a thick wall which is then case with a finishing coat of fine clay. It is essentia that it should be protected from damp and t this end it is usually built on a foundation wa of flint or stone and is given a deeply overhanging roof of thatch. It was the most cheaply available building material in Dorchester and it was used for utilitarian structures as well as for the cottages of the poorer inhabitants. The most instructive, as well as the most accessible example, is the boundary wall to the north of Willoughby House. Here the casing has fallen away to reveal the stone foundation and the lines of the successive layers, each of which had to out before the next layer could be applied. The remains of two similar boundary walls c be seen in the yard of the Fleur-de-lys. The two rectangular structures in the fields to th west of Watling Lane are also built of cob as the original forge in Pratts Yard. The appropriately named Cob Cottage on the orth side of Malthouse Lane probably dates om the nineteenth century as did 8 Rotten w where the cob was replaced when the ouse was reconstructed in 1982.

Both of these are quite large cottages and it necessary to look elsewhere to see how the oouring class was housed in Dorchester in e nineteenth century. Some of them lived in e brick terraces which had appeared on the uth side of Watling Lane before the middle the century. The terrace facing east across e allotments was built shortly afterwards. oert Terrace to the north of the footpath tween Samian Way and Bridge End was ghtly earlier and now survives only as a few indow openings in a stone garden wall. other terrace was formed in the second half the century out of the Malthouse on the uth side of Malthouse Lane. All these rraces were relatively small and provided a inimum level of accommodation in each unit. e individual detached cottages which were ing built at about the same time were not ry much more spacious. 69 Watling Lane is e of the larger examples with a central trance, two ground floor rooms and two tic rooms, and a single large chimneystack ating only one ground floor room and aced outside the house on the eastern ble. Its position parallel to the lane on a rrow strip of garden suggests that it was ilt on common land taken from the roadside rge. This was not an uncommon practice d it is documented in Dorchester from at ast the early seventeenth century. It was rried out under licence from the lord of the anor, which enabled him both to control its owth and to derive a small extra revenue. 71 atling Lane and 22 Bridge End, both mediately adjacent to the east, seem to ve had a similar origin.

By far the largest collection of cottages built the waste can be seen around the green at e south end of Bridge End. As the name plies, this was the approach to the original dge over the River Thame. The present ndsome stone bridge was built a hundred rds or so upstream to the designs of the Irish chitect Francis Sandys between 1813 and 15, and these cottages were presumably

erected shortly afterwards. They are roughly constructed of a variety of materials including poor-quality timber, rubble stone and brick, and they provide a vivid and precious picture of the housing standards of the ordinary nineteenth century villager. There is no conformity in the position of their single chimneystacks, but they all provide the same basic accommodation of two small ground floor rooms and an upper storey squeezed into the roof space.

Apart from the cottages of the poor, the nineteenth century saw very few significant architectural changes in Dorchester. The boom years of the eighteenth century had provided a stock of buildings which were solid enough to withstand any wholesale alterations influenced by changing concepts of taste. Indeed, the few buildings that were erected were conservatively designed to confirm with the standards that had been established in the previous century. Only the important group of public and institutional buildings inspired and

69, Watling Lane.

Cottage in Bridge End.

Thatched Cottage, Wittenham Lane.

largely financed by the Revd. W. C. Macfarlane ran counter to this trend. He was Rector from 1856 to his death in 1885, and he commissioned the designs of his buildings from the best known architects of his day. A new vicarage was built in 1857 to the Gothic designs of David Brandon, who had designed St Mary's Church, Wallingford, shortly before. The Girls' and the Infants' schools which Macfarlane founded on the west side of Queen's Street in 1872 were designed by no less an architect than Sir George Gilbert Scott, who was also responsible for the adaptation and extension of the eighteenth century house on the High Street now occupied by Hallidays, to form a missionary training college in 1878. The fanciful timbered and tile-hung house on the opposite corner of Queen Street was part of the same complex and must have been one of Scott's last commissions for he died in the same year.

The twentieth century has been comparatively kind to Dorchester's architectural heritage. The ribbon development along the Abingdon Road and the modern housing estates to the east of the High Street are for the most part decently hidden away and do not impinge greatly on the historic core. Only the extraordinarily insensitive development of Beechcroft on the west side of the High Street and the group of four houses between Bridge End and Samian Way stand out as representatives of the worst excesses of the 1960s and 1970s. The steel and glass house raised up above the flood level on thin legs to the south of the early nineteenth century toll house still has the ability to shock, some twenty years after it was built for the local architects Donald Morrison and Julia Feilding. It is saved from the unforgiveable folly of its position in front of the Abbey by the quality of its crisp detailing and the enveloping screen of willow trees. It is possible that future historians will see it as one of the more significant architectural contributions of the mid-twentieth century to the continuing story of the buildings of Dorchester, but for the time being its uncompromising self-confidence is out of tune with the more introspective mood of the 1980s.

The River Thames and Day's Lock, looking north from Wittenham Clumps, about 1875 (Taunt photo).

# Dorchester Today

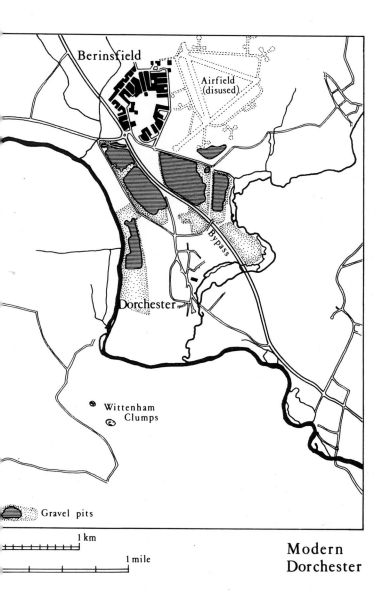

Berinsfield

Airfield
(disused)

Bypass

Dorchester

Wittenham
Clumps

Gravel pits

1 km

1 mile

Modern
Dorchester

**Raymond Nichols**

Dorchester is surprising. Those of us who live here have become accustomed to the looks of astonishment as visitors come to the Abbey for the first time. But the surprises continue as they discover the ancient and prestigious business establishments and picturesque houses of our historic village. As they visit the charming little museum, housed in the old monastic guest house, astonishment grows. Neolithic crop marks; Roman remains; Saxon burial grounds — what next? The very building in which the story itself unfolds is discovered to be the schoolroom of 1652; the children's pencil boxes still there and evidence of the sharp penknife of one of the first pupils clearly seen on the wall panelling.

However, the story of Dorchester begins much earlier than that as this book has made clear. My purpose is to try to describe what this incredible accumulation of surprises means to the present population (of 980), how the life of the community is enriched by them and what kind of values and experiences emerge to shape our future.

Given that the baptism of the King of Wessex took place here; given that much of the life of the medieval church in Wessex and Mercia was centred on Dorchester from 634 to the late eleventh century, how does that affect our community life now and how do we celebrate the historic role of the place which is now our home?

Firstly I could say that we value and treasure that rich history — it is important to us. The things that happened here we believe to be important things in the life and development of our nation and people. We are therefore active in creating interest in them and encouraging new ways of helping others to enter into them. The monastic Guest House, as well as housing our museum, is still the place where visitors are made welcome, travellers refreshed and the friendship of our village offered (all, I hasten to say, with the enthusiastic commendation of Egon Ronay). But it is more than just 'catering' for visitors; it is a continuation of the ministry of countless generations who have lived and worked and worshipped God here. Many members of our village community have become 'guides' in what we call a 'Ministry of Welcome'. Many bake cakes, prepare and serve food, do duty in the museum, tend the gardens, clean and polish, meet groups of schoolchildren and older people who come to our village. This not only surprises our visitors but has a profound effect on the style and quality of life of those of us who live here, whether they have any personal commitment to the Christian faith or not. There is therefore an unusual depth and purpose in our village life.

Secondly, we do, from time to time, focus on particular historic events and give them meaning and significance for our present day world. The first Sunday in July has for some years now been our 'Pilgrimage Sunday'. Congregations from many churches and different denominations gather on Churn Knob at Blewbury, where St Birinus is thought to have preached on many occasions, for a picnic after the morning Services. The walk to Dorchester in the afternoon is often done by 700-800 people and the Pilgrimage Service in the Abbey is always packed, with hundreds sitting on anoraks and sweaters, children covering the chancel floor, the Salvation Army band in splendid form and the heads of Roman Catholic, Anglican and Free Churches welcomed by a fanfare of trumpets. A barbecue in the riverside garden of the Roman Catholic presbytery rounds the day off. But it is not just the commemoration of past history; it is the joyful expression of gratitude for that past and a resolve to be more worthy of what we have been given. The warmth and friendship of the occasion remain as a lasting inspiration to all who share in it.

In 1979 the Bishop of Winchester led a group of 70, which included some from Dorchester, in a commemorative walk from Dorchester to Winchester. The See of Wessex (and the bones of St Birinus) was transferred to Winchester 1300 years before. On this occasion we carried each day a processional cross, commissioned by the Dean and Chapter of Winchester Cathedral. The designer, David John, had visited the Abbey seeking inspiration. He found it in a rough block of

stone from the long ruined shrine of St Birinus. Without doing anything to it he incorporated it in a remarkable cross now in the Cathedral. From photographs of the stone he had etched profiles of its shape in the arms of the cross. Each night, as we slept, the cross slept too. But each morning as we set off, the light caught the different surfaces and the cross came to life again. At the end of the week when we took it into Winchester Cathedral some could scarcely be persuaded to leave it. As we had walked we had thought of the founding of the Christian church throughout the countryside around us but again it was not simply an attempt to re-enact the past, but to enter into the spirit of pilgrimage; love for one another in common commitment to a high purpose and in gratitude for all God's gifts. Such events leave indelible marks on a community and give an unusual dimension to the life of a village.

Thirdly we have in the Abbey one of the most beautiful and inspiring venues for musical occasions that any artist could possibly wish for. For well over twenty years choirs and orchestras have performed and plays have been produced which have widened experience and appreciation of such things to a quite remarkable degree. From some of Britain's leading orchestras to local amateur groups; from discerning concert-goers to proud parents of school choirs, the Abbey has become a setting in which the things which matter most in life have been given tangible expression. To be told, as I often have been, by experienced professional artists, that they have never played or sung better in their lives, gives one a powerful reminder of the spiritual quality of the place.

For forty years the people of Dorchester fought for a by-pass. The most frequent remark heard from our visitors has always been "I have passed through the village for many years but this is the first time I have stopped". It wasn't easy to stop when a huge container lorry was filling your driving mirror and you weren't sure how to get off the High Street. Now, seeing the Dorchester Abbey signs, people make a conscious decision to come. The High Street is gentle and quiet; you can park easily and wander around the village in

peace. The result is that more people come than ever before and we are increasingly finding that they tell others and come back themselves.

Is not this vast and beautiful Abbey church and its surrounding gardens and buildings an enormous maintenance problem and financial burden on a small village community? We have always set our faces against aggressive demands for help from our visitors, in the belief that if others come to know its secret they will share our love for it all and do what they can. For the rest we can only rely on its spiritual worth, its great architictural beauty and its profound historic significance being recognised and valued. We do not believe in feverish fund-raising activity. In a perfectly ordinary village community coping with the same problems as everyone else, people must not be made to shoulder abnormal burdens or made to feel guilty about not doing so. The worship of God as our Father and the praise of him as our Creator and Redeemer has been offerd here for 1,350 years. We would like that to continue.